CLAUDIA

The Story of Colonel Harland Sanders' Wife

by

Edward G. Klemm, Jr.
Author, I WONDER WHY
Co-author, Settles/Klemm THE CLAUDIA SANDERS
DINNER HOUSE OF SHELBYVILLE, KENTUCKY, COOKBOOK

Courier-Journal Lithographing Company
Louisville, Kentucky

Copyright © 1980, by Edward G. Klemm, Jr.

Printed in the United States of America

All rights reserved. No part of this book may be reproduced in any form without permission, in writing, from the publisher, except by a reviewer who wishes to quote brief passages in connection with a review in a magazine or newspaper.

Library of Congress Catalog Card No. 79-56639

ISBN 0-89144-102-6

DEDICATION

Dedicated To Our Mothers,

Roberta K. Klemm, Nancy Ledington and Margaret Sanders

ACKNOWLEDGMENT

I am grateful to Colonel Harland Sanders and to Claudia Sanders for giving me so freely of their valuable time to supply me with the facts and information needed for writing this book, and for their patience in reviewing the completed manuscript.

I also wish to acknowledge my deep obligation to Colonel Joseph Lawrence for his excellent advice and professional help in editing the manuscript.

I am also indebted to my mother, Roberta K. Klemm, for her encouragement and assistance.

Edward G. Klemm, Jr.

Louisville, Ky.
July, 1979

PREFACE

It has long been said that behind every successful man there stands a woman. In the case of Colonel Harland Sanders the woman is Claudia, his wife.

The story of the Colonel is well known and his successful rise to fame and fortune is a tribute to the free enterprise system of the United States.

But his wife's story is far less known, and I feel it should be told. She was more than just an inspiration. She worked with him in the preparation of his recipes and in the promotion of his business in its earlier years.

You have read about him. Now read about her.

CLAUDIA

Claudia Sanders

A farm in Knox County, Kentucky, had the honor to be Claudia's birthplace. Early in the day of September 7, 1902, Nancy Elizabeth Ledington said to her husband, "Jerry, I think the time is near. You had best go fetch the midwife."

Indeed, the time had come. A few hours later Claudia Ledington shared her birth with her twin sister, Nellie, preceding Nellie into this world by about two minutes.

The day was a crisp one. Jerry Ledington built a log fire in the fireplace of the bedroom of their spacious and rambling farmhouse. The chill was driven from the air, and Nancy and the two little ones were warm and comfortable beneath the quilted covers which almost hid them from sight as they rested on the wide, cherry four-poster which had been given to Nancy by her parents.

The midwife's work was finished but she did not want to leave them until she was certain the mother and the little ones were 'doing well.' After that she would turn their care over to the father who was so excited over the fact that his wife had just presented him with twins he could hardly contain himself.

"Quit pacin' up and down," chided the midwife in an attempt to calm him. "Stand still long enough to see your new arrivals." She laughed, looking down at the mother who was holding the infants now bundled snugly in their swaddling clothes. Their little eyes were squinted shut and their little faces looked very red against the background of the clean, white bedclothes. But the mother's eyes were open and sparkling as she looked up at her husband. The two of them shared their happiness.

The midwife began to feel like an intruder. She looked out the window at the wide fields which stretched from the house to the distant hills. The summer was over and the harvest season was approaching. The fields, like Nancy Ledington, seemed to be resting after their labors of the summer. The midwife turned and looked down again at the mother and the two babies and said, "It has been a bountiful summer."

Claudia's father, Jerry Ledington, was an industrious and successful farmer, and she had come into a family that, while not wealthy, was what was called "well-fixed." The farm of over two-hundred acres was well tended by the elder Ledington and the sharecroppers who helped him work it.

Just as the trees of the farm were rooted in the soil so also was Claudia's family deep-rooted to the land. Her great-grandfather on her mother's side was named Jesse Sasser. He had come to Kentucky with his wife and had settled his family in Laurel County before the War Between the States, and from her earliest childhood Claudia heard stories about the war and about this great-grandfather who left home to fight with the Union Army. She was to learn of his adventures and of his death in the fighting somewhere in Tennessee or Georgia. The family never was able to learn the details of his death nor of the incidents surrounding it. His body was never recovered and his end has remained a mystery to this day. All of these stories she heard were to give Claudia a feeling of belonging to, and being a part of, the great heritage of Kentucky.

Then, too, the farm was situated not far from the famed Wilderness Road and the Cumberland Gap. The Wilderness Road, which had carried so many pioneers and early settlers into the west and into Kentucky in their search for their own promised land, passed a few miles to the north of the Ledington farm and traces of the trail were still to be seen. To the southeast was the Cumberland Gap, the famous gateway to Kentucky.

The Wilderness Road followed a trail blazed by Daniel Boone who had been employed by the Transylvania Company to open a road to its new possessions in the lands lying in the area which was to comprise most of what became the Commonwealth of Kentucky and part of Tennessee. This trail, or 'trace,' which crossed into Kentucky by way of the Cumberland Gap originated at a fort called 'The Blockhouse' on the Watauga River in North Carolina. This road had the far-reaching influence of opening the entire West to the pioneers of that day and in increasing numbers they followed the routes of Daniel Boone and Dr. Thomas Walker, the man who named the Cumberland Gap after the Duke of Cumberland. Dr. Walker is reputed to have built the first house erected by a white man in Kentucky. This log cabin stood on the shores of Swan Lake near Barbourville and the site is not many miles from the house where Claudia was born. Being brought up so close to these significant landmarks of pioneer history naturally affected Claudia and gave her pride in being a Kentuckian.

In her imagination Claudia could envision her ancestors as they trudged along these frontier trails. She had many times heard the story about her great-great-grandfather Glass who was living in Virginia when the War Between the States broke out. He owned a good farm with a fine house and barns and was a man of means. Life seemed good to him and his family and all was going well until one day a raiding party of rebel soldiers swept down on his farm and burned his house and barns and killed most of his cattle and hogs. This was a severe blow. One day he was prosperous; the next he was ruined.

Knowing he must start all over again he decided to do so in the land to the west. He gathered his small family around him and told them of his plans to move into the land of Kentucky. All agreed but one daughter who begged to remain in Virginia to wed her lover. She was given permission to do so and remained behind with the blessing of her family which then started out on foot with a small wagon load of precious belongings, two horses and a few cows bought with the proceeds from the sale of the ravaged farm. The family crossed the Cumberland Gap and made its way along the Wilderness Road to the spot in Laurel County which became the new farm homesite. Shortly after arriving in Kentucky Claudia's great-great-grandfather con-

Left to right: Taken when Claudia was about twelve years old. Nellie (Claudia's twin), Claudia, Sally, the Mother with Jimmy on her lap, Bill, Allene.

tracted typhoid fever and died. But his widow, in true pioneer fashion, continued the work he had started, and with the help of her sons, the family soon became self-sufficient.

Claudia came to feel a closeness to the soil and to the trees and flowers of the beautiful land. It were as if she belonged. Little did she know then that fate was instilling in her the qualities which would enable her one day to grace the title, Colonel Claudia Sanders. The pioneer background of both her parents gave Claudia the physical strength and stamina to carry her through the years, and her careful and Christian upbringing developed in her the traits of character which were to be so useful in her later life.

Today, when speaking of her family in those early years on the farm she says, "We were a happy family." The smile on her face when she says this is a tribute to her parents. It is also a tribute to her great-aunt, Elizabeth Glass, who was an inspiration to her and her brothers and sisters.

Elizabeth Glass was a schoolteacher who did not marry until rather late in life. During her single years she spent a great deal of time with the Ledingtons and entranced the children with her stories of the heroes of history and literature. Her stories fired in Claudia a burning desire to learn and to accomplish great things for herself when she was grown.

Claudia especially remembers 'Aunt Elizabeth' telling the children about the little princesses who were rescued by knights in shining white armour who carried them safe from danger to a sparkling castle where they lived 'happily ever after.'

"And remember, little girls," Aunt Elizabeth would often say at the end of her stories, "Somewhere in the world there is a white knight who will come to you someday to protect you and care for you and with whom you will live happily ever after".

This would delight the little girls and they would laugh and giggle each time they heard it. Claudia, deep within herself, wondered if somewhere there really was a white knight. Would she ever meet him and could it be that he would take her to a castle to live happily ever after?

When Claudia and her sister were born there was only one other child in the family, an older sister, Allene, eighteen months old. The large, white farmhouse seemed too big for a family of only five persons, and Claudia and her sisters spent hours roaming through its many rooms as soon as she and Nellie were old enough to walk. But the family was a growing one and this house and others they were to live in over the years saw the birth of fourteen children in all, including another set of twin girls born when Claudia was twenty years old.

As in most families, the eldest child, and in this case the three eldest, Claudia, Allene and Nellie, were called upon to help in all the family activities from being little mothers to the younger siblings to doing the milking and tending to other farm chores. This activity and responsibility built confidence in Claudia, and if we are to search the reasons this young girl grew into a resourceful, steadfast woman we cannot deny the benefit of those early years of farm life.

While it is true that life in the mountain country of Kentucky in the first decades of the twentieth century was hard, Claudia and her family enjoyed a comfortable life. Although the farm was in the mountainous part of Kentucky it consisted of an unusual amount of acreage of flat bottom land which made it a very fertile farm and a valuable piece of property. It was well stocked with cattle and pigs and there was a large flock of chickens which supplied eggs Nancy Ledington could sell to a nearby general store. This gave her ample pocket money for things she might need. Food was plentiful and there was always an abundance of good things to eat. The only things the family lacked were the luxuries offered by the big cities. These were never really missed and the family found its pleasures and happiness in itself. In the evenings, all would gather around the organ and listen to Nancy play their favorite hymns and some of the classics which were in the few songbooks resting on a table in the parlor. Occasionally, Claudia's father would surprise the family by bringing with him on his return from Corbin or Barbourville a new record for the gramaphone. These were highlights in the life of the growing family, for by this time Claudia's first brother had been born and was christened William Franklin Ledington.

CLAUDIA

Claudia's father liked horses and kept quite a few good riding horses on the farm. Each child was given his or her own horse on reaching an age old enough to be able to care for it. Claudia loves to remember how, on Sunday before breakfast, the children would go into the pasture to round up the horses for the ride to church later in the morning. They always rounded up the horses before dressing for church as the grass was usually wet from the early morning dew and they had to conserve the few Sunday clothes each possessed. Then, after breakfast and after attending to the chores which could not be neglected, the family set out for church. The father and mother and the very young children would ride in the buggy followed by the older children on horseback.

"When there were quite a few of us riding horseback," Claudia laughs, "we looked like the cavalry descending on the church."

Within a radius of about twenty miles from the Ledington farm were four churches which rotated their services, each church holding services once every four weeks.

"Two were Baptist Churches and two were Methodist," Claudia says. "But the folks of the neighborhood attended them all with equal feeling. In fact, for most of us the Sunday trip to church was more than a religious experience; it was a social event. After working hard all week and seeing only members of your immediate family it was most pleasant to meet your friends and neighbors. Everyone in the area looked forward to Sunday."

Claudia recalls how delighted she was when her mother told her and her twin sister that they were to witness the ritual of foot washing. This rite was carried out on the first Sunday in June of each year at the Union Baptist Church near Cane Creek.

"I was very happy and proud riding my beautiful bay mare, Star Blaze, to the church the day I was first permitted to watch this ceremony," she says.

Claudia had heard of the ritual many times in the years before and now was able to watch her parents and the other grown folks of the congregation walk to the front of the church, the men on one side and the women on the other. She saw them remove their shoes and stockings and place their feet in the little metal basins on the floor. A deacon for the men and a woman of the church for the women would then "wash" the feet and dry them with a large towel which was tied around their waists.

"How thrilled I was that day," she says, "to see that colorful ceremony. I can still hear the preacher who, before beginning the rite, quoted John, saying, 'If I, then your Lord and Master, have washed your feet; ye, also, ought to wash one another's feet'."

The bay mare, Star Blaze, on which she rode to church that Sunday, is the horse that stands out most vividly in her memory.

"We children loved our horses," Claudia says. "We took good care of them and were not afraid of them and they were not afraid of us. We all became expert riders and would hold races in the fields to see who had the fastest horse. And you might be surprised at how often we girls beat our brothers," she added with a smile.

But her carefree days were not always free of care and at an early age she learned how to handle a hoe and to work in the garden to help her mother grow the vegetables they ate and canned. She learned to clean the kerosene lamps that lighted their house at night and how to fill them with coal oil and to trim the wicks so they did not smoke when they burned. Until her brother was old enough for the task, it was the chore of Claudia and Nellie to keep the box of firewood in the kitchen well supplied to feed the cast iron stove on which her mother cooked their meals.

"For years we did not have electricity," Claudia recalls. "As I grew older and learned to read I poured over magazines and read about life in the big cities and of houses with electricity and of the magic it brought to living. But we were far out in the country and not ever having had electricity we did not miss it nor the conveniences it brings to the home. But my sisters and I were aware of the way other people lived and we vowed that some day we would have our own homes with electricity."

Some distance from the farmhouse Claudia lived in before she was old enough to go to school was a large hill that boasted an orchard on its slope. Above this orchard and on the crest of the hill was a gravel pit that years before had been worked as a quarry but which now stood bare and stark like some bruise on the rural landscape. It was in this gravel pit that Claudia, Nellie and Allene spent hours playing. One of their favorite pastimes was building houses out of the gravel and bits of rock that littered the ground. Some of these houses they made were quite elaborate and were modeled after the mansions the girls saw pictured in the magazines they were still too young to read.

"We would spend hours in this gravel pit," Claudia tells us. "We would outline the houses with small pebbles and build chimneys with fireplaces and put small sticks in them for fire logs. Rocks were our tables and chairs. We would take leaves and make little baskets of them and place them on the tables of our play houses. The tops of acorns made excellent cups, and small, flat rocks served as plates and saucers. How we enjoyed playing there!" she sighs.

-2-

One day Claudia's mother called her and her twin sister Nellie and told them that in a few days they would accompany their older sister, Allene, to school.

"It's time for you to start learning," she said, and added. "I'm sure you will like Mrs. Beets."

Now Claudia had heard her older sister talk about Mrs. Beets and she knew her mother was referring to the woman who was to be her teacher for the next several years. But Nellie had never heard of Mrs. Beets and she whispered softly to Claudia, "Mrs. Beets? Is she red?"

"Of course not, silly," Claudia giggled. "That's just her name."

A few days later, dressed very carefully, Claudia and Nellie walked with their sister to the school house to begin a new phase of their lives. They had to get up very early for they faced a two and one-half mile walk to the one-room schoolhouse at Cane Creek.

Claudia did not know what to expect when she entered the building. She had, on occasion, seen the school house from the outside and, at times, had heard the children inside as they recited for Mrs. Beets. But she felt very small and lost when she entered the large room. It was a typical one-room school house, painted a glistening white on the outside. The inside walls, however, were unpainted and at first Claudia had a feeling of disappointment as she looked about her. But this feeling did not last long. There was too much activity going on for her to let her mind dwell on such things as unpainted walls. In the room, some seated and some standing, were about eighty boys and girls from the age of first graders like Claudia and Nellie to eighth grade pupils.

The voices of the children confused Claudia and she held on to Nellie's hand and followed her older sister, Allene, to a seat at one of the desks which were fastened to the floor in rows. In the front of the room and near the teacher's desk were three benches which she was to learn later were for the children of the class called upon to recite or to use whenever they were to receive special instruction from Mrs. Beets. During these periods of special attention to one particular grade Mrs. Beets saw that the other children were kept busy doing the assignments she had given them. After finishing with one class Mrs. Beets would send the children to their desks and call upon another group to come forward for its period of special instruction.

Claudia was relieved when Mrs. Beets finally called the boisterous group of children to order and quiet descended on the room.

"The one thing that impressed me so much that first day was the huge pot-bellied stove which was in the center of the room and near where I was sitting," Claudia recalls. "There was no fire in it, but it looked so big to me that I wondered if I could sit so near to it in the wintertime. But Mrs. Beets, whose first name was Maggie, did not give me much time to think. I heard my name called, and then Nellie's. Mrs. Beets told us to move to another part of the room where the first grade students were to sit."

Settling herself in the seat of one of the small desks, Claudia looked about her. The room seemed filled with desks, as indeed it was for it had to accommodate up to a hundred little scholars. Each desk consisted of a flat top which raised up exposing a compartment for holding books and notebooks. This top was attached with small hinges to a narrow strip of wood which was grooved to hold pencils and pens. At one end there was a round hole to hold a bottle of ink. The seat in which the student sat was attached to the front of the desk directly behind it.

Claudia laughs as she tells us, "These seats got higher and the desks larger as the grades progressed from the first to the eighth grade.

"Mrs. Beets was a kindly woman, and I knew from the first day that I would like her," Claudia continues. "She seemed to understand children and she made me feel at home. Discipline was no problem for her. Not only did she know how to handle the children, but in those days all of us knew why we were there and we wanted to learn. Occasionally she would have trouble with one of the older boys, but this was rare and I do not recall her ever having a serious discipline problem."

Claudia laughs. "My sister, Allene, was a headstrong one and now and then she would have a run-in with Mrs. Beets. The trouble was that our great-aunt Elizabeth had spoiled her a little. But I will say this for Allene, she had spunk and would let no one get the better of her. One day while we were walking to school Allene was carrying a large basket of eggs mother was sending to the general store we passed each morning. Some boys we knew met us as we reached this store and one of them began to tease Allene. This angered her to the extent she took an egg from the basket and threw it at the leader of the boys, splattering his shirt front with egg yolk and shell. I'll say this, that boy never bothered Allene again."

One might think that a two and one-half mile walk would be a task for two little girls. But Claudia and her twin sister were inseparable and always happy in each other's company and as long as they could walk together the trip to and from the little white schoolhouse was a pleasure for them both. Being in the same grade they used one set of books between them and with the exception of that part of their arithmetic lesson which required pencil and paper they studied their lessons as they walked. The woods and fields heard their voices as one would ask, "Who discovered America?" "Columbus," the other would reply. "When?" asked the first. "In fourteen-ninety-two," came the answer. Or, perhaps, one would ask, "How do you spell teacher?" "T-e-a-c-h-e-r," came the reply.

Claudia feels she owes a great deal more to Mrs. Beets than just appreciation for the knowledge she gained from her about the mundane subjects of grade school. Mrs. Beets was more than just a teacher; she was also a moral inspiration. Every morning before starting classes and after she had called the children to order, she would begin the day with a prayer, read from the Bible and sing a hymn. There was no piano or other instrument in the one-room school, but each desk had its songbook. After telling the children which hymn they were to sing, Mrs. Beets would set the pitch by blowing on a pitch pipe which the children laughingly called 'the tuner,' and raising her arms would direct them in their a cappella performance.

"Mrs. Beets did not end her moral teaching with the daily prayer and hymn," says Claudia. "She continued to instill in her pupils the ethical principles of life by pointing out moral lessons to be learned in their studies of history and literature. Not only by direct teaching, but by setting an example herself, she taught the pupils the value of truth and honesty and the benefits of helping others and being kind.

"Although we may not have known it at the time, this training was invaluable to us," Claudia goes on. "Not long ago, at a meeting of the Business and Professional Woman's Club of Kentucky, I heard a speaker talk on this very subject. He said that the schools of today should get back to teaching fundamentals and the basic ideas of right and wrong. The speaker went on to say that he felt the wave of corruption among men of power who were well educated and who were supposed to be trained to be leaders was due in great part to this lack of moral training in their childhood and, especially, in their early schooling.

"Of course," she adds, "moral training should begin in the home. Fortunately, my brothers and sisters and I benefited from getting this training both at home and from our early years in grade school under Mrs. Beets."

School was not all dull studies in those days. At Christmastime there was a tree to decorate and gifts to give other children and gifts to receive. Then, there were the Christmas plays in which a chosen few took part and performed before the rest of the students.

"Sometimes, if we had an unusually good play we would invite boys and girls from other schools to visit us and see our performance," Claudia says.

When Claudia was in the eighth grade she attended the school at Mt. Olivet. That year, instead of giving a play, the students performed a series of acts on the order of a variety show. Claudia's role was to sing a solo. Her song was "Nearer My God to Thee." She was to sing this dressed in white and was supposed to act very much like an angel while performing.

"Just before I started to sing and as the pianist who accompanied me struck the opening chords I looked out over the audience and saw a young man get up from his seat and dash out of the room. I recognized him as Charles Price, a young man with whom I had developed a deep friendship. In fact, a few years after this, he and I were married. But this night, when I saw him run out of the room, my heart sank. I knew I must go on with my performance and somehow I was able to do so. When it was over and I had left the stage, I peeked out from behind the curtains and there he was back in his seat. When I met him after the show was over, I asked him what on earth had gotten into him to make him leave the room. I'll never forget the look on his face as he told me, 'I didn't think you could sing it, and I couldn't stand to be in there if you didn't give a good performance. We laughed about this many times in later years.

"But what I liked even more than the plays," she goes on, "were the box-lunch picnics the school gave each fall to raise money. These were very popular in the neighborhood and drew large numbers of people. For days we girls would spend hours decorating the box we were to donate as our contribution to the school. Some of these we made were quite elaborate. We would take a cardboard box and cover it with colored crepe paper which we sewed on the boxes so that it hung over the sides in little ruffles. We would then add a ribbon with a large bow and sometimes even put an artificial flower on the lid. Inside this box we would put the lunch. This lunch consisted of two of everything. There were usually two apples, or two bananas, or two of some other kind of fruit. Then there would be two servings of some kind of meat with one or two kinds of vegetables and two pieces of either cake or pie, together with two bottles of some kind of soft drink. For some reason or other the meat in my lunches was always fried chicken. As I look back on it now, I think fate may have been trying to tell me something," she puts in with a smile.

"Now the reason the boxes contained two of everything was that they were to be auctioned off to the highest bidder who would then eat the lunch with the person who had prepared it. The person preparing the lunch always put her name on a slip of paper and placed this in the box with the lunch. After selling the box, the auctioneer would read out the name from this slip of paper. In this way, the name of the person who prepared the lunch was not supposed to be known until after the box had been sold.

"These lunches were really very successful in raising money for the school. If the boys suspected one of the lunches to have been prepared by one of the more attractive or popular young ladies the bidding would become frantic and go quite high. Some of these boxes would sell for as much as forty or fifty dollars, and that was a great deal of money in those days."

Claudia's school days were brightened now and then by mild bits of excitement such as the times birds would fly into the classrooms through the open windows in the springtime and in early summer. The windows were never screened and this would happen quite often.

"Those poor birds would fly around in desperation to get out of there," Claudia relates. "But this would only amuse the children, and then some of the bigger boys would try to catch the bird which was vainly trying to get out of what, to it, must have been a horrible predicament. At these times the teacher was helpless to control the noise and confusion and took it in stride and often even tried to help shoo the bird back out the door. When this was finally accomplished the class would quiet down and studies go on as usual. But, really it was great fun, and I always enjoyed the diversion.

"But not all diversions were as pleasant. One day, during recess, a sudden storm came up, and before the children could get back into the classroom a bolt of lightning hit and split asunder a large tree near the front of the schoolhouse. Two boys standing in the doorway were knocked to the floor and several children in the schoolyard were thrown to the ground. Fortunately, no one was seriously injured, and before long we were all back at our desks and immersed in our studies. But this experience was a traumatic one for me and, until I was grown, whenever there was a thunderstorm I would cover my head with a pillow if I could and wait until the storm was over. But that was when I was a child, and happily, I outgrew this fear.

"And I want to say this about the teachers in those days," she goes on. "They not only taught us our lessons but they acted as caretakers of the schoolhouse as well. They always had to arrive at the school before the first student showed up. In the wintertime this meant they had to build a fire in the big, pot-bellied stove so the school room would be warm by the time the classes were to begin. If one of the children got sick or was injured they assumed the role of nurse and almost that of the doctor. They more than earned the small salaries they were paid."

Due to the fact the family moved from the farm on which she was born, Claudia attended the school at Cane Creek only through the fourth grade. Her school years from the fifth to the eighth grade were spent in the school at Mt. Olivet.

"Although I enjoyed my years at the Mt. Olivet school," she tells us, "my happiest memories of school are those with Mrs. Beets.

"My first experience with moving came when I was four years old. My mother had been reared by her grandmother after her own mother had died when she was very young and her grandmother was like a mother to her. When Grandmother Sasser became too old to take care of herself my mother prevailed upon our father to let us move to another house so she could take care of her grandmother. The house we moved to was a larger one than the one in which I was born. It was less than a mile away so the move did not seriously uproot us, and we children could still play in the same fields and woods we had been enjoying.

"Although this move was something of a hardship for my father, he adjusted to it for he was a very understanding person. He knew that my mother loved her Grandmother Sasser dearly and that she wanted to be able to take proper care of her. As I look back on it now, this willing self-sacrifice on father's part was just one way of his living his Christian moral life and I am sure this example he set had its good influence on my sisters and brothers and me."

CLAUDIA

In the country there was no place to go for entertainment and nothing to do after chores were finished, so it was up to the children to find their own amusement. There were times Claudia's mother would have to go to the general store which was about a mile and a half from the farmhouse. To reach this store she had to walk down a country road called Sled Road Branch. The 'Branch' in the name was derived from the fact that, for the most part, this road followed the bed of a small creek and the rocky roadbed was nearly always covered with shallow water. Now because of this poor road, whenever Claudia's mother went to the store, the children knew she would be gone for a rather long time and they had the run of the house. These were the times they enjoyed themselves.

"As soon as mother had left, we would get out some of her dresses and put them on," Claudia says. "We pretended we were grown folks and would strut around the house in what we felt was a dignified impersonation of an adult. To make the dresses fit us snugly we would roll up other clothes and stuff them under mother's dresses to fill them out. When we tired of this we would climb onto the straight-backed, cane-seated dining room chairs and rock them back and forth. We had learned that if we did this properly the chairs would 'walk' across the floor. We pretended the chairs were horses and would beat them with imaginary whips.

"My sister, Nellie, liked brown sugar very much and many times when mother was away she would climb on a chair and reach onto the pantry shelf to take down the large bag of brown sugar kept there. One day she dropped a bag on the table in the kitchen. The bag burst and the brown sugar spilled all over the table top. Resourceful Nellie immediately walked to the stove, opened the oven door and took out the large baking pan that was always stored there. She scooped up the brown sugar and put it in the baking pan which she then placed back in the oven. Later that day, mother started a fire in the stove but fortunately discovered the pan in the oven before the heat had melted the sugar. We laughed about this for years. Mother knew our play was harmless. She understood children and seldom punished us when our playful antics led to awkward situations. As I have said, we were a happy family in those days."

-3-

About the time Aunt Elizabeth was relating her fascinating stories to the children, especially the one about the White Knight, a young man by the name of Harland Sanders was working as a fireman on a railroad locomotive. This young man did not in the least resemble a White Knight. In fact there were times when he was of quite the opposite color. Although he did wear white overalls and gloves, unhappily he could not keep them from becoming covered with coal dust and soot. But a remarkable metamorphosis was to take place one day and, while this young man might not become a knight in shining armor, he would be transformed into a knight in a white suit and, indeed, was to bring to Claudia the fulfillment of all her early dreams. But this was still far in the future and neither he nor Claudia had the least inkling where the road of life was to lead them.

For the young man in 1906 to become a railroad fireman was the culmination of his highest aspirations.

The Colonel says today, with a faraway look in his eyes, "I'll never forget the first day I fired an engine. Just to be around those steam locomotives was all I could ask for. I know it is trite to say steam engines of those days were like living beings, but I can think of no better way to describe them. They seemed to breathe and pant as they stood on the rails waiting for the engineer to pull his throttle to send them charging down the track. I have a pretty vivid imagination and in those days, just like today, I had a lot of ambition and I would lean out the cab window and look down the track ahead of me and somehow I knew those two shining rails were taking me farther than just to the next station."

While the Colonel was looking forward then to where he was headed it must be admitted that he had already come a long way for a sixteen-year-old who had left home only some four years earlier to make his fortune in the world. He had been born near Henryville in southern Indiana on September 9, 1890. His father died when he was about five years old, leaving his mother with the task of rearing him, his brother, Clarence, and his sister, Catherine. Both his brother and sister were younger than he. Like Claudia, he lived on a farm and helped with the chores and with the upbringing of his brother and sister. And, like Claudia, he too had a mother who instilled in him the Christian virtues of the Ten Commandments. She took the children to church and to Sunday school and taught them by example as well as by formal instruction to be truthful and honest and to follow the Golden Rule. She told them to avoid tobacco and alcohol and gambling in all its forms.

"You might think she wanted my brother and me to be ineffectual little gentlemen. But don't you believe it," the Colonel says. "She wanted us to be men as well and taught us how to look out for ourselves and to face responsibility and never to run from a fight or trouble. And she instilled these principles in our sister, as well.

"We lived by mother's teachings," he goes on to say. "We didn't need any of the thousands of laws which the country has passed just to enforce the Ten Commandments. All we had to do was follow her guidance."

When Harland was twelve years old, his mother remarried and the family moved to Greenwood, Indiana. But the young boy did not get along very well with his step-father, so he announced to his mother that he was leaving, and it was with tears in her eyes that she helped him pack a battered suitcase the day he set out on his own.

"I was only twelve years old at the time, so I'll admit my eyes were wet too," he says.

For about two years he worked for a farmer by the name of Sam Wilson. "But I was beginning to tire of farming and a relative got me a job working for the streetcar company in New Albany. I guess you might say this was a step in the right direction for a young person who wanted to be a railroader. I was riding on rails even if they weren't train tracks and for the time being I was content and happy.

"Most young boys in those days went through a stage of wanting to be a policeman, or a fireman, or a railroad engineer," the Colonel goes on to say. "My love was the railroad and I was in a seventh heaven when I got my first job working for the Southern Railroad. It wasn't a very glamorous job; I was a blacksmith's helper and didn't get any farther than the roundhouse. But I was around the engines I loved and I was happy. Shortly after going to work I was given the job of doodlin' ashes and I never was able to figure out if this was a promotion, or not. This job consisted of cleaning out the fire boxes of the locomotives when they came in off a run and in getting them ready for their run the next day. I was now actually working on the engines themselves and could climb over them and I was enjoying myself more than ever before.

"Then all the happiness in the world opened up to me the day a fireman failed to show up for work and I was asked to go in his place. I did such a good job on that run that I was given the job of fireman full time. I knew this time it was a promotion!"

And so began for the young man who was to become the Colonel Sanders of Kentucky Fried Chicken fame the journey down the long road filled with adventures and which finally merged with that road taken by Claudia Ledington when he and Claudia were married in 1949. Little did either know in that year their greatest adventures were ahead of them and that for the Colonel life would begin at sixty-five.

Now, on that journey to the year 1949 the Colonel discovered that his life was a series of exciting and surprising events, having its share of ups and downs, of successes and failures.

During these years the Colonel tried to settle down into a life with a steady job and one that would not take him away from his family. He was now married to his first wife and they were beginning to raise a family. He worked for a while on the Pennsylvania Railroad and then, in a effort to better himself with a white-collar job, he sold life insurance. But it was hard for him to stay in this routine and these years saw more vicissitudes than times of happiness. It was during this time of his life that he suffered his two greatest tragedies; the death of his son and his divorce from his first wife. But the Colonel is a fighter, not only with his fists, but with moral courage as well. He kept on going.

And then one day he opened a gas station in Corbin, Kentucky. In time, this opened the door to the restaurant and motel business and was actually the start of the road to the success he gained later in life.

Having started with nothing but a domineering determination to amount to something, the Colonel has little use for those who can, but will not, help themselves. But he is also aware from what he saw in his earlier years that there are many people who are the victims of circumstance and who are unable to help themselves. He realized these fellow men must be assisted by those more fortunate. "If it were not for the grace of God, I might be walking in their shoes," he philosophizes.

This deep understanding and sympathy for people has led him to become one of the greatest philanthropists of the day.

In fact, he has made his Canadian franchise business a completely eleemosynary operation. When he sold his fried chicken franchise business in 1964 the sale did not include the franchises in Canada. Four years later he incorporated the Canadian business into the Harland Sanders Charitable Foundation and transferred all holdings of stock to that corporation. A Board of five trustees operates and conducts the affairs of the corporation.

The Colonel tells us, "An unusual feature is the distribution of monies. Each franchisee sends to the Board his royalty of five cents per chicken sold. The Board deducts a sum equal to the ratio of expense of operation from this remittance and then a check is written in the name of the charity designated by the franchisee. This check is sent to the franchisee so that he may present it personally to the charity of his choice. Each franchisee is free to select the organization to receive his particular donation. This might be a boy's club, church, school, mission, or any other suitable charitable organization.

"These checks total to nearly a million dollars annually," the Colonel goes on to say. "The Harland Sanders Charitable Foundation is not of a character to build up and retain a large sum of money, but must distribute its earnings as they are computed and determined."

Today, the Colonel continues to make all television and radio commercials for the Canadian company and, naturally, he has endeared himself to his Canadian friends.

On his eightieth birthday a one-hundred dollar-plate dinner was given in the Colonel's honor. The proceeds from this birthday party amounted to fifty thousand dollars and this sum was presented to the Muscular Dystrophy Association.

But the thoughtful Colonel is also one who believes that charity begins at home and he has seen that his own relatives are well cared for, even giving as a wedding present the franchise business for the state of Florida to his daughter, Margaret.

Today, the Colonel will surprise you with his wit and wisdom. He has all the worldly goods he needs but this has not changed him from the person he has always been.

"You see," he will say, "I learned early in life that you had to make your money before you could spend it. I never spent my paycheck before payday and after I had worked for a dollar I knew I could make it work for me. But don't think I was obsessed with working. I never took my troubles home. That's as bad for you as running with booze-hounds."

The Colonel has come a far way from the day he left home as a twelve year old to make his fortune in the world and has even come a long way since the day he and Claudia were married in 1949.

But, as the Colonel says, "It's not where you start from, but where you finish that counts."

But now let us turn our attention back to Claudia and her adventures during these years the Colonel was struggling as a young man.

-4-

On April 30, 1921 Claudia Ledington and Charles Price were married. By this time all the children of Nancy and Jerry Ledington had been born and the family was now a large one. The fourteen children and the parents 'really filled up the house' as Claudia puts it. Besides Nellie, Claudia's other sisters were Allene, Sallie, Thelma, Kotha, another set of twins named Mary and Joyce, and Rose, the youngest, who was the 'baby' of the family. Claudia's brothers were William Franklin, James, Hiram Finley, (whom they called H. F.), Robert and Julian.

Since Claudia was the first among her sisters and brothers to marry, the coming wedding was the source of much excitement in the family, especially among the younger girls who were most romantic-minded. All looked forward to the wedding day with joy, most of all Claudia herself. Like most brides-to-be Claudia was happy in the belief that a great future of happiness was ahead of her, not knowing that she would discover one day that the step she was about to take would bring her the first tragedy in her life. But at that time thoughts of unhappiness were far from everyone's mind. Plans were made and talked over and a feeling of joviality permeated the house. Claudia's sisters spent days in decorating each room while her mother sewed on the beautiful white wedding gown Claudia was to wear. By the time the night of the wedding arrived the house was tastefully adorned with large bows of white ribbons skillfully placed here and there about the rooms and on doorknobs. Besides the ribbons in the parlor, vases of wild flowers rested in the center of small tables and on the organ. In the dining room a table was set and waiting for the happy gathering which, just before seven o'clock in the evening, convened in the parlor for the nuptial ceremony. Claudia's immediate family was there, with the exception of Allene, who was working as a nurse in Lexington and whose duties prevented her from leaving the hospital. Only a few of Charles Price's relatives were able to attend the wedding. His parents were old and unable to make the trip to the Ledington home, but had sent their blessings.

The evening was warm, and the slight breeze which blew through the open windows made the bows of ribbons tremble somewhat like the nervous bride and groom as they stood before the minister and said their vows.

But at last the ceremony was over and the quiet room exploded with a stir of activity as everyone shook hands with the groom and kissed the bride. Claudia remembers how this was broken up when one of the very young children said plaintively, "Can we eat now?"

Charles Price was a farmer at the time he married Claudia and since his father was very old and unable to do much work the responsibility of tending the family farm fell mainly on Charles shoulders. Because of this the couple had to forego a honeymoon. It was spring and the farm work was demanding.

"Overnight I went from the carefree days of my youth into the busy life of a housewife," Claudia recalls. "But I did not mind. What bride does?"

Shortly after the marriage, Charles announced to Claudia suddenly and rather abruptly, that he had decided to quit farming and go to work in the coal mine at Kettle Island, a small community a few miles to the northeast of Pineville.

"What about the farm?" Claudia asked, somewhat taken aback by Charles' unexpected announcement.

"I've arranged for someone to take my place," Charles assured her. "I've talked this over with my father and he is agreeable to it."

Now Claudia did not really mind making this move, as her twin sister, Nellie, had, in the meanwhile, married a man by the name of George Ray and was living at Kettle Island. In fact, it was George

Ray, a miner himself, who had influenced Charles to come to the mine to work.

"The work is hard," George Ray said to Charles, "but the pay is good and the hours are definite. You do not have to work day and night as you do on the farm."

Although Claudia did not realize it at the time, her husband's move of giving up the security of the farm and the steady future it afforded them was a harbinger of his actions to come and was an indication of traits in his character which were to cause her heartaches in the future. But for now, life seemed to move smoothly. Claudia, while living away from her family for the first time, was near her beloved sister, Nellie, and she felt secure and content. Besides, she was recovering from an emotional shock she had suffered shortly before moving to Kettle Island.

Her parents had moved to a home near Robinson Creek after Claudia and Charles were married and it was there that tragedy struck them. On that day the air around Robinson Creek had become unusually still and, as Claudia's mother put it later, she had the eerie feeling of impending disaster but dismissed it with the one word, "nonsense."

But it was not nonsense, for just before four o'clock in the afternoon the air began to stir. Suddenly and without warning, the wind started to blow with furious force. Mrs. Ledington looked out the window and to her horror saw coming directly toward the house a black, funnel-shaped cloud. Disregarding any danger to herself she rushed out of the house and ran toward the barn calling to her husband who she knew was inside currying the horses. Her voice was drowned out and the words literally torn from her mouth and hurled away by the force of the wind which by this time sounded to her like the roar of a freight train only a few feet away. Caught between the house and the barn, Nancy wrapped her arms around a small sapling and, in a state of terror held on while she watched as the roof was blown off the house by the tornado, only to see this catastrophe followed by the collapse of the barn which buried her husband under its broken timbers. How she survived she does not know. But in less than three minutes it was over and rain began to fall. Nancy ran screaming toward the ruins of the barn calling to her husband.

"Jerry! Jerry! Are you all right?"

She heard a moan and then the voice of her husband as he called, "Here I am, Nancy. I almost made it out of the barn when it went over."

Nancy hurried toward that side of the barn which had faced the house. Looking under the twisted tin of the metal roof, she could see her husband. He was lying face down just inside and seemed to be pinned to the ground. She was able to crawl under the roof and discovered that he was held firmly by a large beam which had fallen across his back just below his shoulder blades. There was only one thing to do, and that was to get him out of the wrecked barn and do so in a hurry. How she was able to do it she could never explain. Somehow she found the strength to raise the beam just high enough for her husband to drag himself out from under it. Later, whenever she talked about this, she would say, "God helped a little."

As soon as Jerry was safely outside, Nancy looked again in the direction of the house and exclaimed in a voice filled with anguish, "Heaven help us! The children!"

"Go to them. I'm all right now. Just let me lie here for a while. Forget me and go to them!" her husband urged.

Nancy rushed to the house and to her great relief found her children safe, although they were huddled together and trembling with fright as tears ran down their cheeks.

Seeing the children were safe, Nancy hurried back to her husband who by this time was able to get on to his feet and stagger on shaky legs into the house and out of the rain which by that time had drenched both him and Nancy to the skin. Jerry had suffered three broken ribs and multiple bruises, but beyond this, he was not injured.

Unfortunately, the storm and heavy rains which followed washed out bridges and roads and Nancy and Jerry were unable to contact the only doctor in the area who lived at London, Kentucky. But the true pioneer spirit of native Kentuckians came to the surface, and Nancy was able to nurse her husband back to good health, with the aid of Claudia who came to lend a hand.

Unfortunately, although Jerry Ledington had carried insurance on the house and barn, the policy did not cover tornado damage, and he was forced to sell the property at a loss and return to one of the houses he owned in Laurel County.

The only other after-effect of this experience to the family was that whenever a storm came up Claudia's mother would leave the area or, if this were not possible, she would retire to an inner room of the house and sit there in great distress until the storm had passed.

For a while after the tornado, Claudia's husband worked seemingly content in the mine at Kettle Island bringing home a steady paycheck. But then one day Claudia's father came to Kettle Island to see them and said to Charles, "We are leaving the Laurel County home and moving back into the house where Claudia was born. If you and Claudia would be agreeable to it, I should like for you to live there. It will make me happy and it will be somewhat like a belated wedding present."

To Claudia's surprise, Charles readily agreed. She did not know it but due to his restless nature he was already beginning to tire of his job in the mine and he wanted a change.

Moving back into the house she had been married in was a pleasant move for Claudia. Although it meant leaving Nellie, it also meant she would be near the rest of her family. And, besides, she liked living on a farm and preferred it to the life of a small town as a miner's wife. No longer would she have to live with the extreme apprehension that she might hear that long blast from the mine's whistle signalling that disaster had struck. Too often she had heard the stories of wives who waited long hours while their husbands were trapped deep underground by a mine cave-in.

Still, it did not enter her mind that her husband's ready agreement to give up his job indicated a restlessness of spirit and a lack of desire to fully accept responsibility.

Claudia and Charles lived on the farm in Laurel County for about two years in seeming contentment. But farming very quickly brings to the surface the character of a person. Claudia began to notice traits in her husband that had, perhaps, been unseen before because she was a young bride full of hopes and aspirations for the future.

Claudia has only kind words for Charles. "He was a very pleasant and affable person—the kind of man you like to be around," she says. "He could play music and he could sing well. Had he been able to control his carefree and irresponsible attitude toward life all would have been well. But the carefree and irresponsible attitude controlled him and the result was that he did not take responsibility seriously."

The farm began to show the effects of his neglect. Gradually Claudia noticed this and sensed the first faint feelings that something was wrong with their marriage. Being a person who took life seriously, she did not let herself neglect her work as a housewife, nor could she condone her husband's neglect of his work. Slowly the rift between them widened, and they separated.

But, somehow, they could not stay separated and two years later they were back together again, this time living in Corbin, Kentucky.

When Charles was offered a job in the Tennessee Rolling Mills in Knoxville they moved to Tennessee. Charles seemed to like his work at the mill and Claudia's hopes rose. Perhaps now, she thought, their marriage was on the road to success.

While they were living in Knox County, Kentucky, a son, Ray, had been born. Now, as a coincidence, a daughter, Billie Jean, was born to them in another Knox County—Knox County, Tennessee.

"I thought having the children would inspire Charles to stability, but it didn't," Claudia reflects. "Now, I am one of those people who faces bare facts. We were so different in our makeup that I knew we could never be really happy together. So, in 1930 I suffered the first tragedy in my life; I divorced Charles, knowing this to be the only solution to our problem. With my two children, I moved back home to live with my parents in Kentucky. Charles and I remained friends. We just had to face the fact that we were two opposite personalities and could not be happy together."

Of course, good character is not developed in a life where there is no trouble. Just as gold must experience the fire of the furnace before it can become the valuable and useful metal which men treasure so highly, so, also, must the human heart be tried by adversity to become a thing of value. Just as an easy life is not always the best life, neither is one with some tragedy necessarily the worst life. Stalwart Claudia, who always faced her problems and found their solution, now looked ahead determined not to let the unfortunate years which had passed be a stumbling block to her future. And she vowed she would never let her children see her in anything but a happy mood.

She did find happiness living again with her parents. She kept busy helping her mother with the housework and in devoting herself to giving her children the same type of upbringing she herself had received. Soon, life became tranquil again.

-5-

Many writers, including John Heywood and William Shakespeare, have referred to the "ill wind that blows no man to good." And this is true in the case of Claudia. The year 1929 is always to be remembered as the year in which the Great Depression began, and this was indeed an ill wind for nearly all Americans. But for Claudia the Depression was in some ways a good wind in that it was the major factor in her meeting the man named Harland Sanders. The famous crash of Wall Street affected the whole economy of the United States. Plants and factories closed down and men and women by the thousands were thrown out of work. Among these many thousands was Nellie's husband, George Ray, who had left the mines and was working for the Louisville and Nashville Railroad at the time of the Crash. George Ray was not the kind of man to sit around and wait for the soup kitchens to open. He was a hard and willing worker. When he heard that a man in Corbin by the name of Harland Sanders needed someone to help in his service station, he applied for, and got, the job. It did not pay what he had been earning on the railroad but it paid something, and in those days it was that "something" that counted—the difference between a small salary—and no salary.

It was about this time that the Colonel decided to branch out in his business activities and open a restaurant. You see, Sanders was a courageous fellow and he did not let even a Great Depression scare him.

In the corner of his service station was a small room that at one time had been used as a storage room. Since no use was being made of it at that time, the Colonel decided to put in a table and a few chairs and see if he could sell meals to his customers as well as gasoline. Especially, he was thinking of the tourists who drove from north to south and back again like migrating birds. He needed a waitress and George Ray saw that his wife, Nellie, got the job. The Colonel's food was good, and soon the business of his restaurant began to eclipse that of his service station. He realized he needed more help.

"Nellie," he said one day. "Do you know anyone who could help you?"

"I have a sister who might be able to work part time," Nellie replied. "I'll bring her over to meet you."

The fateful day Nellie introduced Claudia to Colonel Harland Sanders seemed like any other day. But what a change it was to make in both their futures!

"Harland Sanders seemed like a very nice man," Claudia says in looking back on their first meeting. "I really thought no more of meeting him than I did of meeting anyone else. I did not seem to make a great impression on him, although I felt he liked me. At least, he hired me and told me I could go to work for him, starting the next day.

"At first the work was part-time only. Nellie often worked in the kitchen as cook and it was mostly at those times I helped out waiting tables, or I should say table, for at this time there was only one large family-style table, and all the customers sat around this one table. Later, as business improved, my hours increased until I finally found I had a full-time job.

"There was never a dull moment working for the Colonel," Claudia says with a smile. "He was a human dynamo, always on the go and infecting everyone around him with his tireless energy. He was always active, always doing something, and doing it with enthusiasm. He was never satisfied with the way things were. He was constantly making changes, all with the purpose of improving business. To him, the customer might not always be right, but he was always the customer, and the Colonel was out to please him and give him service that would bring him back. Harland always knew that a satisfied customer is the best advertisement and a sure way to increase business. The really important thing about his manner, then and today, is that it is natural. He had no affected manners and what he does to please people comes from his heart. He did not have to read a book about how to deal with people; that knowledge seems to have been born in him.

"Because I was a great deal like him in many ways, I felt attracted to him. I was a willing worker, thrifty and industrious, and uncomplaining. I guess I admired him for years without actually realizing it. And, as I found out in later years, he had observed qualities in me he liked all during the time I worked for him. He often remarked later how he had noticed I was dependable and industrious and that this had impressed him very much."

Things were indeed lively in the little one-room restaurant in those days, and the monotony of waiting tables was often broken by odd and humorous incidents. One evening, Claudia saw one of the customers laughing. He was sitting at the large dining-room table with another man. Claudia noticed him point to his salad and say something to his companion who roared with laughter.

Now Claudia did not like the idea of someone laughing at her salads, so she walked over to the customer and asked him if anything were wrong.

The man looked up at her and, still laughing, said, "No, there is nothing wrong. I had asked the young girl who waited on me to bring me the tossed salad with the dressing on the side. When she brought the salad she pointed to one side of the bowl and told me she had put the dressing on that side of the salad."

This made Claudia laugh too. Recovering her composure, she took time to tell the inexperienced young waitress who was helping out that evening that "dressing on the side" meant to bring the dressing in a separate dish so the customer could put it on the salad himself.

Claudia will tell you that for a man of the Colonel's caliber the restaurant could not long remain a one-room affair. Business, in fact, was booming, so the Colonel, with his usual self-confidence decided to buy the property across the road from his service station and build not only a restaurant, but a motel as well.

"In those days most motels were sorry looking tourist cabins and were not attractive places," Claudia says. "So the Colonel built his motel as a tourist court with all the rooms and the restaurant under one roof."

With an eye to business and to let the public see how attractive his motel rooms were, the Colonel arranged it so that in order to go to the ladies' rest room the women customers had to go through a sample motel room. This room which was never rented was furnished exactly like all the other rooms in the motel, and the floor, rugs, and maple furniture were always kept spotlessly clean. A sign near the door explained that this was a sample room and that all rooms in the motel were exactly like it. The Colonel figured that if you pleased the ladies they would influence their husbands.

One day a man went into the ladies' rest room by mistake. After he had left, Claudia discovered he had dropped his billfold on the floor of the rest room. She did not count the money but she could tell that the wallet contained a considerable amount. She took it immediately to the Colonel who left it at the counter of his restaurant with instructions to give it to the customer if he returned.

The next morning on coming to work, Claudia learned that the customer had come back in a state of distress and retrieved his wallet.

"He did not leave a reward," laughs Claudia. "But the Colonel had been given an example of my honesty and that was reward enough for me."

Not all incidents were humorous, however, and there was the time a customer could have gotten Claudia in trouble had it not been that the Colonel knew her character and trusted her. By this time, the restaurant was larger and boasted several tables and a counter on which rested a cash register. In those days, all drinks such as soft drinks, coffee, tea, or milk cost five cents. Whenever several customers came in together only for something to drink as is often the case in roadside restaurants, Claudia would collect a nickel from as many as four or five customers at a time. Rather than ring up a series of five-cent sales on the cash register, she developed the habit of collecting all the money and then ringing it up in one grand total. One day a customer with a group of men gave her his nickel and noticed that she did not ring up the sale. Not waiting until the others had paid their checks, he walked over to the Colonel and said, "That girl at the cash register is knocking down on you."

Now the Colonel was aware of the way Claudia rang up these sales and in no uncertain terms he told the customer he did not know what he was talking about.

"It certainly made me feel good to see him take up for me like that," Claudia says. "Thank goodness he knew how I operated the cash register and trusted me. Many another person might have fired me, but not the Colonel."

The Colonel was a great believer in signs and over the roof of his service station located next to his motel was a sign reading "Sanders Court." It also announced to the public that the rooms had tile baths and steam heat.

Besides this sign and the one in the sample motel room there was a message on the menus of his restaurant which read "If the food isn't good, don't pay for it." The Colonel felt that if the customer legitimately did not enjoy what was placed before him he should feel free to call the waitress and complain. Naturally, the Colonel did not expect a customer to eat a good dinner and then get out of paying for it simply by saying that it wasn't good. But this is exactly what happened one evening. Four women tourists came to the cash register and said the food wasn't good and they didn't think they should have to pay for it. "After all, isn't this what the menu says?" said one of the women. The Colonel walked over to the table they had just left expecting to find plates of partly eaten food. Instead, the plates were clean! The women had eaten every bite of their meal! Nevertheless, the Colonel told them they did not have to pay for their dinners. At least, he would stick by his word even if he knew these customers were taking advantage of him.

CLAUDIA

"You know," he says today, and now he can laugh about it, "those women stayed in my motel that night, but in the morning they ate their breakfast in another restaurant down the road. They were too ashamed to eat in my restaurant that morning.

"You'd be surprised at what you run into when you deal with the public," the Colonel continues. "What some of my guests did made those women look like pikers. People would take towels, pillows, blankets, sheets, and even lamps out of the motel rooms. Sometimes, if we discovered this before they had left and were eating breakfast, I would call the sheriff and we would search their cars and recover the loot. I never had anyone arrested. Just told them I didn't want any more of their business."

Corbin, Kentucky was a wild town in those days. Moonshiners operated in the hills and in nearly every hollow. They and the bootleggers who bought the liquid lightning from them to sell in the town were often the Colonel's customers and he got to know a great many of them. Claudia, too, came to know many of them by sight, and she often thought of the time she was a child and had gone into the woods with two other little girls. On one particular day they penetrated the forest surrounding her father's farm deeper than ever before. She and the other little girls were only six or seven years old at the time and they were having quite an adventure. Suddenly, they came to a clearing in the woods and saw before them a very strange contraption consisting of copper vessels, a boiler and a coil.

"We had come upon a still," Claudia says. "But we did not have the least idea what it was and we examined it with great interest, especially the copper coil which led from a large container to a jug which was resting on the ground. In a large box, painted white as I remember, were sacks of what must have been grain and sugar. After a while, as is the nature of children, we began to get scared and hurried home, running as fast as we could. We told my mother what we had seen and I'll never forget what she said to us when we asked her what it could be. She said, 'You found a bear's nest. And don't you dare ever go back there again!' "

Years later, waiting on tables in Harland Sanders' restaurant Claudia often wondered if any of the older moonshiners she was serving could possibly have had a hand in operating that still she found in her childhood.

Her mother gave her good advice, and the Colonel will tell you, "This part of Kentucky is feudin' country. You just don't mess with anybody down this way. It can be dangerous to your health."

But city dwellers can learn to be afraid of people, too. This was evidenced one night during a power failure. The lights in the restaurant went out suddenly, and Claudia heard the voice of a terrified woman as she screamed, "Grab your bags, folks! This is a holdup!". The poor woman felt rather foolish when the lights came back on and the other diners looked at her in astonishment.

The Colonel leaned close to Claudia and whispered, "She must be from Chicago."

One night, not long after this, the local chapter of the Business and Professional Woman's Club held its birthday party in the Colonel's restaurant. At the time, Claudia was the Vice-President of the Club and had gone to a great deal of trouble to see that everything was in perfect order for the dinner and the meeting that was to take place. It was to be a gala affair and the members of the Club brought their husbands with them for the celebration. Claudia was especially proud of the cake which had been baked for the occasion. When it was delivered she put it on a cake stand which she placed on a sideboard in the dining room. When all the members and their guests had arrived, the Colonel decided to show them the cake which was to be their dessert. He lifted the cake stand off the sideboard and held out the cake for them to read the "Happy Birthday B. and P. W. C." written in icing on the top of the cake. So the members could read it more easily, the Colonel tilted the cake forgetting it rested on a plate and not in the recessed top of the cake stand. The cake slid off the plate and was the smash hit of the evening—on the floor!

Undaunted, the Colonel looked at the guests and said, "The pie a la mode is on me tonight, folks."

-6-

By 1939, in spite of the Great Depression, the Colonel's motel and restaurant business was doing so well in Corbin, Kentucky that he decided to branch out. Accordingly, he built a motel and restaurant in Asheville, North Carolina, in an effort to cash in on that city's resort and tourist trade. When the building was completed and ready for operation he took with him several of his older employees so that he would have on his staff in Asheville a few who were familiar with his way of managing a restaurant. Among these was Claudia in whom by this time he had a great amount of confidence. He put her in charge of the restaurant. Also, she was to oversee the management of the entire Asheville operation when he was not there to look after things in person.

"Since the Depression was not yet over," Claudia says, "the Colonel, in order to stimulate business, conceived the idea of taking his guests on free sight-seeing trips around Asheville and its environs. There were many interesting places to take them. There was the Biltmore Industries, which produced very expensive woven materials of the highest quality, and the famous Biltmore Estate, along with other places of interest. Sometimes, he would even drive his guests more than twenty miles to Chimney Rock. I think he enjoyed these outings as much, or more, than his guests did. He liked people and was always happy doing something for someone. He insisted his guests be given the opportunity without fail to take these little tours and if he weren't available he made sure one of his employees was on hand to take his place as a guide."

But then, just about the time the Colonel felt the Depression should be easing, along came the Second World War and rationing. Gasoline rationing, at first, did not hurt his business as much as did food rationing, and while the shortages obliged him to close his restaurant in Asheville he was able to keep his motel going for a while.

During this trying period, the Colonel received a request from a national restaurant chain based in Seattle, Washington, to come there to take charge of the food division of its operation. The Colonel had met the owner of this chain at a meeting of the National Restaurant Association and had impressed the food chain owner very much. So, with business slowing down almost to a stop in Asheville, the Colonel welcomed this fortunate turn of events.

"He asked my sister, Joyce, Marie Moore, who lived in Corbin, and me to accompany him. We were all glad for this opportunity, and I took my daughter, Billie Jean, with me so she would have the experience of traveling and living away from home for a while," Claudia relates.

While the Colonel was in Seattle he left his motel in charge of a woman who lived near it. With automobile travel as light as it was then, one woman could easily handle the business as only a few guests checked in each night.

At the end of nine or ten months, the Colonel returned to Asheville and continued running his motel there for another year.

But, then more trouble came his way. His restaurant in Corbin burned. Since his business in Corbin was the more important one, the Colonel sold his motel in Asheville and proceeded to put up a new building in Corbin. And as in most similar cases this building was bigger and better than the old restaurant and motel. The new restaurant could seat 140 people. The Colonel had decided that his future lay not in the motel business, but in food and food service.

Claudia will tell you that it was during these years that two tragedies struck the Colonel. One was the death of his only son, Harland, Jr. The other was his divorce from Josie, his wife of thirty-nine years. These tragedies, much like the tragedies in Claudia's life, tempered him just as Claudia's tragedies had tempered her.

For a while he was depressed, but his spirits finally took over and he found surcease in hard work.

"My son was just over twenty when the streptococcus infection took him," says the Colonel. "But I consoled myself in thinking that he had lived twenty years of a happy life, and there was no way of knowing what the future might have held for him and that this way he might have escaped a great deal of misery. It might not have been good thinking, but it helped me and for that I was thankful."

Just as in the case of Claudia and her former husband, the Colonel and Josie remained good friends after the divorce. "I was unhappy that we had not been able to make a go of it, but it was better to part than to continue living unhappily as we had for the past thirty-nine years," the Colonel says.

Claudia tells us, "It was about a year and a half after the Colonel and Josie divorced that he proposed to me. He is very outspoken—not rude or blunt—just outspoken and he said something to me one day like: 'I've been married and you've been married so let's us get married.' It was so like him to put it this way that I think I said 'yes' before I even realized it.

"And this time I had a real honeymoon," she goes on. "We went to New Orleans and spent about ten days there seeing the sights and eating in the many excellent restaurants in the city. We had a grand time making a lovely holiday out of those ten days. We spent hours walking up and down the colorful streets of the French Quarter and took boat rides on the Mississippi as well. This was in November of 1949. Neither of us was young, but we had as much fun as a couple of kids. This will always be one of the happiest memories of my life."

Success isn't born in a person. A man might be born with the physical and mental capacity for success, but the actual success itself is the result of many factors. In talking with the Colonel a person can easily see how he had become the successful entrepreneur who not only reached the pinnacle of success in his chosen field but who has become a legend in his own lifetime. The Colonel was given by nature the physical stamina needed to enable him to put in the long hours of hard work which faces every person who strives to reach a goal. In his mental makeup, the Colonel was gifted with the ability to accept failure when it came his way and to shrug his shoulders and keep going in spite of everything, supported only by his sense of humor. You see, not everything the Colonel did met with success.

As active as the Colonel was, and getting into one undertaking after another, he could not expect all his ventures to be successful. And then there were times he would enjoy a success on one hand while suffering a failure on the other. For instance, his motel and restaurant operation in Asheville was forced to close because of the coming of World War II and food and gasoline rationing. Being in a resort area and not located directly on a heavily travelled highway this business suffered from the effects of the times. On the other hand, the motel and restaurant business in Corbin was booming as it was located on one of the busiest north-south highways in the eastern United States which, even in wartime, carried a great deal of traffic. There were the soldiers and their families traveling from home to camp, business men with war contracts in their pockets, as well as government officials of high and low rank. His restaurant also benefited from the fact that it was situated in a small community in a rural area and non-rationed foodstuff could be obtained from the neighboring farmers so that a varied menu could be offered to his customers.

Besides his Asheville project, other enterprises of the Colonel's had failed. The Colonel analyzed why they failed and learned from this so that later he could correct his mistakes. There is one worthy mark of an intelligent person and that is to be willing to admit a mistake and profit from it. What some people might call making a mistake the Colonel called keeping faith with himself. He would never compromise with principle. He had lost one job while working on the railroad because, as a union member, he took up for an underdog. "I would lose a job every day in the year before I would fail my fellow man," he says emphatically.

Also, being a success, means turning an obstacle into an advantage. When his motel business in Asheville was in a state of decline, and finding himself with time on his hands, he grasped at the opportunity to go to Seattle to work for the large restaurant chain. There he learned that he was cut out for the food industry and that his talents lay with food and food service.

Again, when his motel and restaurant in Corbin burned he did not wring his hands and lament his fate. Instead, he went to work and rebuilt a new and better establishment which rose Phoenix-like from the ashes of the burned out building.

Many know how, but few know when. And it is the ability to know this "when" which can make or break a business venture. Of course, the "when" is often a matter of luck and there is no denying that chance often plays a major role in the success or failure of a business venture. The Colonel could not have foreseen in 1939 that a war and rationing were to put an end to his Asheville enterprise.

Nor could the Colonel foresee that some twenty years after building the new restaurant in Corbin that the country would begin its massive road building program under the Eisenhower administration. Word of coming events gets around long before the events themselves and one day the Colonel saw the way the wind was blowing. Information was out that an interstate highway was to be built near Corbin but was to bypass the city itself. This meant that future north- and south-bound traffic would no longer pass the Colonel's restaurant and motel. This north-south traffic was the lifeblood of the Colonel's operation and without it business at the motel and restaurant would decline alarmingly. This naturally reduced the value of the business and the real estate and the Colonel knew he could no longer expect to realize from their sale what he might have gotten only a couple of years earlier. Aware that no one who understood the restaurant and motel business would be interested in buying the property and that it would no longer profit him to continue his operation in Corbin, the Colonel put his business and the real estate up for sale at auction.

"At least, I got enough out of it to pay my debts and now, at sixty-five, I was right back where I had started from earlier in life. I just didn't know what to do," the Colonel says.

Claudia laughs. "The Colonel might say he didn't know what to do, but we who knew and understood him knew that it wouldn't be long before he would know exactly what to do."

How right she was! Turning another apparent disaster into an advantage, the Colonel announced one day shortly after selling the motel and restaurant, "Claudia, now that I have nothing pushing me I am going to put my efforts on my fried chicken."

"What do you mean?" Claudia asked.

"I mean I am going to improve it and introduce it to the public in other restaurants. In other words, I am going to franchise it."

As always, in beginning a new venture, the Colonel waxed very enthusiastic and the air around him became charged with the electricity of his zeal and industry. No sooner did he tell Claudia of his intention to franchise his fried chicken than he herded her into the kitchen and began giving instructions.

"We are going to improve my recipe. I want you to keep a detailed record of the ingredients we use in cooking each batch of chicken. The recipe is good as it is, but I think we can make it still better."

So, for days he and Claudia cooked chicken and kept accurate records of the ingredients used in each recipe they tried out, and of the exact amount of each of the spices and herbs they used. The Colonel recorded the exact length of time he cooked each batch, together with any change he might make in the procedure he followed. He even experimented with new ways of cutting the chicken for frying.

Day after day he and Claudia worked in the kitchen. Then, one afternoon the Colonel turned to Claudia. There was a drumstick in his hand with a bite taken from it. He was chewing and there was a smile on his face.

Claudia tells us, "I could tell by his expression that he had found the flavor he had been looking for. He did not have to say to me as he did, 'This is it, Claudia. Taste it'."

Had Chicken Little known what was happening that day in Corbin, Kentucky, she would have again run around screaming, "The sky is falling!" But chickens, like humans, would have paid her no mind and would have dismissed her antics as those of just another crank. Had she raised her wing with a clenched fist and called out, "Power to the chickens!" they would have paid her no mind.

-7-

Once the Colonel was satisfied with his recipe he immediately went ahead with the business of getting franchises. It was like him not to lose a minute's time getting started in any new venture.

About this time, the Colonel heard of a church convention to be held in Australia. He decided to go there in hopes of getting some inspiration for overcoming his habit of cussing, a habit which had plagued him since he was a little boy. The habit had developed along with his aggressive spirit which was needed in his young days to help him cope with the hard surroundings of his early life. But that need was all past now and the Colonel was determined more than ever to break himself of the unnecessary habit. On the way to Australia he stopped in Salt Lake City to visit an old friend by the name of Pete Harman who ran an excellent restaurant in that city. The Colonel had become acquainted with Mr. Harman at a National Restaurant Association workshop at the University of Chicago some years before. When they met, they learned that neither of them drank and they hit if off right from the start and became the best of friends. So, it was natural for the Colonel to make a stopover in Salt Lake City on his way to Australia to see his old friend. It was during this visit that he interested Pete Harman in becoming a franchisee of Kentucky Fried Chicken. This was the Colonel's first franchise and was a great encouragment to him. On top of this, Pete Harman became one of the Colonel's greatest boosters and helped spread the fame of Kentucky Fried Chicken in those early days when the Colonel could use all the help he could get.

CLAUDIA 45

And now, Claudia's work was cut out for her. While the Colonel is the more outgoing of the two of them and is always on the move, Claudia is more reserved and while she also likes to travel she is also content at home doing the routine chores of housework and now she found pleasure in her new occupation—that of tending to the mixing of the spices and herbs and seeing that they, together with other items the Colonel supplied his franchisees with, were packaged and delivered.

During the early days of their operation, the Colonel and Claudia turned the garage behind their house into a warehouse and workshop. Here Claudia spent her time blending the herbs and spices according to the Colonel's secret recipe. After mixing the ingredients in the exact proportions, Claudia measured out specified amounts of

Claudia at a Christmas Party with the Colonel and M. K. "Bill" Summers.

the finished preparation and put them in cellophane packages the Colonel had made for the purpose.

"Believe you me," Claudia says with a laugh. "Some of those spices made my eyes and nose water until there were times I would think I couldn't stand it. But there was one bright side to this. All during the time I mixed them I never had a cold!"

Besides the spices and herbs, the Colonel supplied his franchisees with glasses, paper place mats, and napkins. On these was printed "Colonel Sanders Kentucky Fried Chicken." This was good advertising and the Colonel was always careful to see that each franchised outlet was well supplied with these items.

Since the garage Claudia worked in was rather small and since she needed all the room she could get, the Colonel's car had to be left outside in the driveway.

"The packages of napkins, place mats, and glasses were rather large. They were long and heavy and I could not lift them completely off the ground by myself," Claudia says. "But I was able to raise one end by myself and rest it over the rear bumper of our car so that I could raise the other end and slide it into the trunk. To do this I would back the car as close to the garage as possible, open the trunk lid, and go to work loading it as best I could. These packages were too large and too heavy to mail so I would drive to the railroad freight depot and send them express.

"This was not easy work, but I did not mind it. It was a pleasure to do for we had found an occupation at a time when everything looked dark for us and it was a project that had every indication of becoming a success."

And she adds with a smile, "At that time we did not dream how great a success it was to be."

Claudia and the Colonel make a well-balanced pair. The outgoing, energetic spirit of the Colonel is tempered by the more relaxed and sedate character of Claudia who, while not in the least timid, is just not as demonstrative in her show of enthusiasm as the Colonel. This balance in their characters has helped them in their life together and has been good for their marriage. If the Colonel should become too enthusiastic and excited Claudia is there to exert a calming influence, and if she is in need of encouragement or stimulation he is there with his exuberance to give her just the lift she needs.

Due to their temperments, each was happy in the work each did to make the franchise operation a success; Claudia, quiet and reserved, working alone in the garage, and the Colonel, outgoing and enthusiastic, on the road meeting people and making contacts and lining up franchises. Indeed the two made quite a pair in those days.

Looking back on the early days, Claudia says, "Strangely, the first franchise the Colonel contracted for his Kentucky Fried Chicken was not in Corbin, in fact not even in Kentucky, but far west in Salt Lake City. Which shows that fate has strange ways of operating. Before long the Colonel's franchise idea was catching on, and while it was hard going for us at first, making great efforts to interest people in the operation, it finally came to pass that people were writing to the Colonel and even coming in person to see him about opening a franchise. Some years later, when we were living in the large house near Shelbyville, Kentucky, it was not unusual to have as many as eight or ten prospective franchisees staying with us at one time. The Colonel likes people and was always glad to have them stay overnight, or for several days for that matter."

Back in the early days at Corbin there were times when Claudia would be well caught up in her work and even have an oversupply of the Colonel's prepared spices and herbs and other items on hand. It was at such times that she would accompany him on his trips to line up new outlets for his Kentucky Fried Chicken, which now was beginning to be known all over the country.

Sometimes on these trips Claudia would do the driving. It so happened that she was driving one afternoon as they started up a long, steep hill near a small town in Illinois. A car in front of them was going very slowly, and the Colonel who has the habit of getting somewhat impatient in such a situation, urged Claudia to pass the car.

"You have to please the Colonel when you are driving," Claudia says with a laugh. "As we were still far from the top of the hill and there was no car coming toward us, I blew my horn and pressed down on the gas pedal, easily passing the other vehicle."

No sooner had she done this, than she heard a siren behind her, and a local police car pulled her over to the side of the road.

"Where it came from, I'll never know," Claudia says. "It must have been hidden for it seemed to appear out of thin air."

The officer in the car, who looked more like a farmer than a policeman, got out and walked up to where Claudia had stopped her car. He asked Claudia for her driver's license which she handed to him.

He looked at it, read her name and address, and then looked at her, saying, "Didn't you see that sign back there?"

Without giving Claudia a chance to answer, the Colonel spoke up. "What sign? There wasn't any sign back there."

The officer turned his attention to the Colonel and said very slowly and deliberately, "There is a sign back there at the bottom of this here hill that says, 'NO PASSING ON THE HILL'."

Well, the Colonel didn't believe this and insisted there was no sign. Finally, he told the officer to drive back down the hill and show them the sign he claimed was there.

"I didn't think the officer would agree to this," says Claudia, "but surprisingly he did, and we ended up down the hill with him pointing to a sign that read, 'NO PASSING ON THE HILL'."

Now this sign the officer was pointing to was very small and was placed on the end of a very long pole. In fact, the sign was so high that if you were not looking for it there was little chance of your ever seeing it. It was so skillfully placed that even if you were looking for it there was a good chance you would fail to see it.

The Colonel and Claudia realized they were the victims of a variation of the "speed trap" used by small communities to get revenue by fining unwary strangers passing through the area.

Claudia tells us, "In a little while we were standing in front of a justice of the peace in a shabby room the officer referred to as a courtroom. The magistrate, who was sitting behind a small desk, asked the officer what the charges were and on being informed, told us we could either pay a nineteen dollar fine and costs or stay overnight and hire a lawyer for a court trial the next day."

The Colonel was justifiably angered and he fussed and fumed telling Claudia not to pay the fine but to stay over and fight it the next day. But Claudia was practical-minded; she knew she didn't have a chance either way. So she argued with the Colonel and finally convinced him the best thing to do was to pay the fine and put it down to experience.

"He agreed, at last," she says. "And we paid the fine and left. But not until after the Colonel told the magistrate what he thought of the treatment we had received.

"You purposely put that sign up so high that no one can see it," the Colonel said, and then went on in no uncertain terms to let the magistrate know his opinion of such a community.

"I was glad to get out of there before the Colonel got us fined for contempt of court," says Claudia with a laugh. "But that old judge just listened to him with no emotion at all on his face. I guess he had heard other people say the same thing on many other occasions and was willing to settle for the nineteen dollars he got out of us.

"When we got outside and were walking back to our car, the Colonel started in again and began telling me what he really thought of the town, the policeman, and the magistrate. He spiced his tirade this time with some of the colorful cussin' he was noted for and which he was trying to overcome. I listened for a while and then told him I was glad he hadn't used language like that back in the courtroom.

" 'Back there,' he grunted, 'it would have cost me money'."

Later on, the Colonel and Claudia travelled thousands of miles in airplanes, going to many parts of the world as well as over most of Continental North America. But never on these travels did they have the narrow escapes like those they had while travelling by automobile.

On one occasion they were driving to Knoxville, Tennessee, to get some supplies for their restaurant in Corbin. The road from Corbin to Knoxville in those days was a well-paved asphalt road but was very narrow. It was also hilly and in many places it ran along the edge of a cliff on one side and a sheer wall of blasted limestone on the other and at these spots it seemed more narrow than it actually was, especially when there was no guardrail for protection as was more often the case than not. On this particular ride to Knoxville the Colonel was driving. As they came to a rather sharp curve in the road the driver of a tractor-trailer approaching from the opposite direction took his half of the road out of the middle and crushed the Colonel's car against the rocky wall where the road had been blasted out of the hillside. Fortunately the Colonel was travelling on the inside lane. Had he been on the outside at this particular spot he would have been forced over the side of a cliff with a drop of approximately one hundred feet. The impact with the tractor-trailer practically took off the left side of the Colonel's car. When the bumping and the scraping was over the Colonel and Claudia found themselves sitting in what looked more like a battered tin can than the fine automobile it had been just moments before. Miraculously, neither the Colonel nor Claudia had been injured. The truck driver, who had been the cause of the accident was also uninjured and his tractor-trailer had suffered only some scratches and dents on its left side.

"As usual," laughs Claudia, "the one to blame for the accident got off the lightest."

After telling the driver of the truck what he thought of him and his driving, the Colonel told Claudia he would get a ride back to the last town they had passed through and come back with a wrecker to tow their car to a garage. Claudia agreed to wait in the car until he returned.

She had been knitting on an afghan as they drove along that day and, in fact, was working on it when the accident happened. So, while she waited for the Colonel to return with the wrecker, she sat in the crushed automobile and began working on her afghan again. Later, after the car had been towed to a garage and she and the Colonel were eating their evening meal in the only restaurant in the small town, she happened to overhear a woman at another table say to her companions, "And then we passed this awful wreck and don't you know a woman was sitting in it knitting just as unconcerned as if she were in her own home. I never saw such composure before in my life".

Claudia remarks, "People have often asked me if I am afraid to fly. I have always felt safer in a plane than in a car. Sometimes someone will ask the Colonel if he isn't afraid to fly as much as he does and when they ask him if the big planes crash very often, he loves to spring the old joke on them and reply with a straight face, 'No. Only once'.

"We have never had any trouble in a plane, but the Colonel was nearly killed once when a bridge he was driving over collapsed. But this happened before we were married and I was spared that worry. But another time, after we were married, we had a narrow escape in a freak automobile accident. It happened before we sold our restaurant in Corbin on a ride we were taking to Somerset, a town located some miles to the northwest of Corbin. It was about nine o'clock in the morning of a beautiful day and we were enjoying the fresh air and the countryside without a care on our minds. On a straight stretch of road we saw a car approaching us which we learned later was carrying four or five drunks who had been out all night and who were in a very mellow condition for that early hour in the morning. Surprisingly, their driving was all right, but just before our cars passed a wheel came off the drunks' car and headed right down our side of the road. This startled the Colonel who was driving at the time. He turned so suddenly to avoid hitting the runaway wheel that he ran off the road and over a fifteen foot embankment. We rolled over on our side and the car rested there with its engine running and its rear wheels spinning as it was still in gear. I found myself crushed between the right side of the car and the Colonel who had been thrown on top of me. He began squirming around and said, 'Let's get out of here!' I heard him try to open the left door, but it was either sprung or was too heavy for him, and he couldn't budge it. I then heard him cranking the window which fortunately rolled down. As soon as he got out of the car he turned around to help me climb out.

But I was busy reaching for the ignition key to turn off the motor as I was afraid it might catch fire and I didn't like the prospect of being trapped inside a burning auto.

"When we were standing outside the car, I asked the Colonel why he hadn't turned off the motor before he got out of the car.

" 'All I wanted to do was get out of there,' he replied in his usual direct manner.

"Speaking of cars," Claudia went on to say. "The Colonel always believed in having good ones and once owned a Cadillac sedan. He had this car at the time he ran for state senator from his district. He was motivated mainly to run for this office because of his belief in temperance and he thought the whiskey interests were getting too powerful in Kentucky. Now the Colonel wasn't too well known in some parts of his district in those days, so he did a lot of personal campaigning and I often went with him. People who aren't familiar with some of the back country of Kentucky cannot visualize what some of the roads are like. But to the Colonel and me who had grown up in this country they were a commonplace. One day we had occasion to drive back into some remote hollows to see some of the 'electorate,' as the Colonel called them and we had to drive up a creek bed which served as the only road into the area. In fact, this creek-bed road reminded me of Sled Road Branch, the road we used to take to go to the store when I was a little girl. I guess we must have looked pretty funny that day in an expensive Cadillac bouncing along the rocky creek bed and splattering water every now and then when the car wheels dropped into deep potholes which held the only water in the nearly dry creek. Anyway, we passed several barefoot teenagers who stared after us in amazement as if they couldn't believe their eyes. I heard one of the boys say to his companions, "What you see when you ain't got a gun!".

"It was after this experience of driving up the creek-bed road that the Colonel made road building a major part of his campaign. 'These counties need roads more than anything else right now,' he would say. 'If we are going to bring progress to this part of Kentucky we need good roads. You just can't bring progress up creek beds.'

"I am sorry to have to say that the Colonel did not win the election," Claudia continued. "We heard that many powerful interests were against him. In his heart I think he was not sorry he lost for he felt he would have had a hopeless battle fighting those interests if he had won.

"The sad thing about his campaigning for good roads is that when the country later on brought its huge road-building program to this area it was this very program that put out of business the one man who had had the vision to see the need for roads so many years before. Of course, I am referring," she adds, "to the time the interstate highway bypassed the Colonel's motel and restaurant in Corbin taking away the tourist trade which was the lifeblood of his business. But at that, this turned out to be a blessing in disguise for it motivated him to go into his franchise business." And Claudia smiles proudly when she says this.

"And to think," she continues, "I would have missed all the fun of helping him demonstrate his fried chicken to prospective franchisees. To do this, the Colonel would take over the prospect's restaurant and while he worked in the kitchen preparing the chicken I would act as hostess. On these occasions I always dressed up in an ante-bellum costume and greeted the customers in as gracious a Southern manner I could assume. For me, it was almost like being in a play and I enjoyed those demonstrations immensely."

The Claudia Sanders Dinner House of Shelbyville, Kentucky. This famous restaurant is Claudia's first franchised operation and is in the building originally built by the Colonel to house the offices of his Kentucky Fried Chicken.

-8-

Claudia Sanders opened her restaurant, The Claudia Sanders Dinner House, near Shelbyville, Kentucky on June 1, 1968. At that time she and the Colonel were living in their large brick residence on U.S. Highway 60. Behind the house the Colonel had put up a sizeable frame building to serve as the offices and storerooms of his Kentucky Fried Chicken operation. When the Colonel sold his business in 1964 the offices were moved to a new location first in Tennessee and then near Louisville, Kentucky. This building became vacant and four years later the Colonel and Claudia decided that she open a restaurant which would be entirely different from the carry-out franchise operation.

No expense was spared in getting the new restaurant ready. It was to be a quality operation featuring not only chicken dinners, but old country ham, steak, and lobster dinners, as well. Tastefully decorated in the Southern tradition, the dining rooms were to be decorated in keeping with the plantation type architecture of the building itself. Emphasis was to be placed not on carry out service, but on dining at tables. Indeed, the Colonel felt new life coursing through his veins. Again he was to be involved in the managing of a restaurant like those he had operated in his earlier years in Corbin.

A few months before opening the restaurant, the Colonel suggested to Claudia that they approach Mom Blakeman of Lancaster, Kentucky, and make an effort to persuade her to be the manager of the Dinner House. Mom Blakeman was well known to restaurant men in Kentucky and was something of a tradition herself. She was loved and respected by all who knew her and had built up an enviable reputation as an excellent restaurant operator. For years she had run her restaurant on the Courthouse Square in Lancaster and had specialized in Southern cooking of the highest quality. The Colonel knew she would be an asset to any restaurant with which she might be associated.

In fact, he says of her, "She was a stickler for quality. She used only the finest ingredients in her dishes and was never satisfied with anything but the best. We knew if we could persuade her to manage Claudia's restaurant she would help make it a success."

When the Colonel suggested to Claudia that they ask Mom Blakeman to come to Shelbyville to work for them, Claudia readily agreed.

The Colonel wasted no time in taking off for Lancaster to talk to Mom. But when he got there he learned that she was in the hospital. Having no idea if she were seriously ill or not, the Colonel hurried to the hospital and with a heavy heart entered her room to find her propped up in bed. She seemed bright and cheerful and told the Colonel she would soon be out of the hospital. Encouraged by this, the Colonel told her the reason for his visit. Mom Blakeman's eyes lit up. She had retired as she was in her late seventies and the prospect of being able to engage actively in business again cheered her greatly. The Colonel sensed this and went on zealously painting a beautiful picture of the restaurant and how nice it would be for her to be associated with Claudia and him. But as he continued talking to her he noticed that her hands trembled a great deal as if she did not have complete control of them and she appeared more tired looking than he had observed when he first entered the room. The Colonel began to have serious misgivings and felt that perhaps he had made a mistake in coming to see her. He squirmed in his chair and began to think of ways to get out of the predicament in which he suddenly found himself. He tried turning the conversation to generalities and hoped he could leave her without making a final commitment. When he finally said good-bye he had the feeling he had left the door open and that if he did not contact her again she would forget the whole matter. On the way out of the hospital the Colonel talked to her doctor who confirmed his opinion that Mom Blakeman would in no way be able to handle a position of grave responsibility.

The Colonel returned to Shelbyville and told Claudia about Mom Blakeman's condition and that they would have to look around for someone else to manage the restaurant.

"Me and my big mouth," the Colonel grumbled, shaking his head. "For a while there I was painting a glowing future for Mom. But I think I saved the day before I left by making everything appear problematical."

The Colonel and Claudia gave no more thought to the matter, thinking it closed. Then one day shortly before the opening of the new restaurant the Colonel and Claudia learned that Mom Blakeman had paid them a visit while they happened to be in Louisville for the day. According to some workmen who were putting the finishing touches on the restaurant, Mom Blakeman had spent a great deal of time going over the building, examining the kitchen and the dining rooms with much interest. The workmen reported that she had told them she was going to be in charge of the restaurant and to tell the Colonel and Claudia she was staying at the motel down the road.

The Colonel and Claudia visited her immediately on getting this information and to their dismay saw that the little old lady had revived and was looking forward to the new interest in her future. Unable to tell her they felt she could not handle the position, the Colonel and Claudia returned home to discuss the matter privately.

"I don't know what to do," the Colonel said. "I do not have the heart to disappoint her."

"I know how you feel," sympathized Claudia. "Whatever we do, we mustn't hurt her."

The Colonel was silent for a long time. Then he spoke.

"You know, Claudia, Mom Blakeman is a splendid person. When she ran her restaurant in Lancaster during World War II she never charged a soldier for a meal. I know there must be hundreds of men today who remember her with affection. She would be worth a lot of money now if she had not been so good-hearted. We cannot let her down. We must find some way to help her. Perhaps we can offer her the position of just being an overseer and greeter of the public. She will add color to your restaurant and will be an asset just sitting near the front desk and talking to the customers. I'll contact her tomorrow and see what I can work out."

The Colonel did just that and for nearly two years Mom Blakeman could be found in her rocking chair near the reception desk of the restaurant always willing to converse with the customers.

The Colonel gave her a "gift" of one hundred dollars a week. When he found out she was paying fifty dollars a week at the motel where she was staying he moved her into a room on the first floor of his own house.

"This room has an adjoining bath, and I had it fixed up to use when I got too old to climb the stairs," the Colonel says. "The room is at the rear of the house and the windows face the restaurant. I put a handrail up the outside stairway to help Mom Blakeman go in and out. She was very happy here and Claudia and I were glad the entire problem had been solved satisfactorily."

Mom Blakeman held her position as "official greeter" for nearly two years. One day, the waitresses noticed they had not seen her for about an hour and a half and in looking for her found her on the floor of the ladies' room semiconscious and lying in a pool of blood. She had fallen and had suffered a severe laceration of the scalp together with a mild concussion. The Colonel and Claudia rushed her to the hospital and saw that she had the best attention. When she recovered she felt unable to continue her work as 'official greeter'. She returned to her home in Lancaster where she died a few years later.

"We all miss Mom Blake," the Colonel will tell you. "She was a tradition and one of the 'old school'. There are few like her left in the world today, and I know that many people, especially the young ones, are just a little better off having the memory of meeting and talking to a person like her in Claudia's restaurant."

The Colonel continues, "There is one story about Mom that stays in my mind. Years ago when she was younger and in the heyday of

CLAUDIA

her restaurant in Lancaster she weighed around three hundred pounds. One of the specialties of her restaurant was her pancake dish which consisted of a platter of what she called her 'thin pancakes' made from a very thin batter rich in butter. In fact, these pancakes were almost like crepes suzette in their richness. They were delicious. One day, a customer who was eating one after another as if he couldn't get enough of them remarked to Mom Blakeman, 'These are mighty good, but don't they make you fat?' The three hundred pound Mom Blakeman whose bulk almost hid the stove she was cooking on, replied, 'Nah. Look at me. I eat them all the time'."

Just as small straws flying through the air show the way the wind is blowing, so small and unobtrusive traits can show the greatness of a person's character.

It has long been the habit of this writer to dine out a great deal, often eating in the same restaurant over a period of many years. The owner or operator of these restaurants naturally would become friendly and would sit at times at his table to pass a few pleasant moments in light conversation. Now this writer appreciates good food and a good restaurant in the Ludwig Bemelmans tradition and was delighted to discover Claudia's restaurant shortly after it opened. The twenty-seven mile ride from his home to the restaurant was through open farm country and was a pleasure in itself and the distance was no deterrent to making the drive almost daily with his mother to eat there. Such restaurants are hard to come by. One day the Colonel, who at that time was not yet a personal friend, came to the table where this writer was eating with his mother and said to the waitress, "These folks have been eating here regularly for a long time. Don't give them a check today. This dinner is on me."

Never before in all the years of dining out was a more generous or courteous gesture ever experienced, and this action on the part of the Colonel was appreciated by this diner more than the Colonel could ever know.

Another example of the thoughtfulness of Claudia and the Colonel came to light when, after watching the little waitresses carry in the heavy trays with the meat course and bowls of eight vegetables served with each dinner, they had carts made so that the dishes could be wheeled into the dining rooms.

"We just couldn't bear to see those little girls burdened with heavy trays," they say, showing again their deep understanding of, and concern for, other people's problems.

What is the charm, the charisma, that the Colonel and Claudia have that makes their restaurant ventures such successes? Of course, the first reason for the success of any restaurant is its food. But in the case of Claudia's franchises it is more than that. Her ventures reflect not only her personality but that of the Colonel as well.

When Claudia decided to open her restaurant the Colonel gave her a great deal of good advice although, of course, she was knowledgeable about the restaurant business herself. It had always been her belief that if a restaurant served good food in clean surroundings and at reasonable prices it would succeed. But her restaurant was to go even further than this. In it she was to serve excellent food in not only clean, but attractive, surroundings. The third item she did not change: she would adhere to the moderate prices, and even in the days of inflation kept prices at moderate figures.

Too often Claudia and the Colonel had patronized restaurants that looked like something out of a picture book with elaborate decor, often enhanced by gold wallpaper, a thick carpet reaching from wall to wall, tables immaculate with their white tablecloths, shining silverware and sparkling crystal and china, and then alas, the worst food possible. "If such an experience hadn't happened to us personally—and often—I wouldn't believe it," says Claudia with a sigh.

Her concern for the restaurant industry compels her to continue. "In Europe many inns and restaurants are family affairs and the business has been handed down from generation to generation. There is pride in the ownership and operation of these places and I think the people of Europe know this and appreciate it. In Europe a little boy will start his career as piccolo and develop over the years into a superb waiter, chef, or perhaps owner of a fine restaurant. In America we have had it very easy and have put our minds on the accumulation of worldly goods. As a people on the move and living as fast as we do in our wonderful country we have not had the time to indulge in the taste for graceful dining on a large scale. It exists here, but the connoisseur must look for it. I am sorry to say it, but it seems to me that the era of graceful living is dying out all over the world. There are still excellent restaurants to be found, but I am afraid they are becoming fewer and fewer as life becomes more and more hectic."

Claudia ran the Claudia Sanders Dinner House Restaurant for quite a few years during which time she and the Colonel made many trips over the United States and to many foreign countries publicising the Kentucky Fried Chicken business which the Colonel had sold and was now owned by a large corporation.

"I began to feel that I was not giving the personal attention to the restaurant that I should," Claudia says. "So we decided to franchise it. This was in 1973. We sold the franchise for the Shelbyville restaurant to Tommy and Cherry Settle. Cherry Settle had worked for the Kentucky Fried Chicken Corporation and was well-known to the Colonel. We also sold the Settles the real estate which consisted of our house and the restaurant building itself. Then we moved to a new home in a subdivision near Louisville.

"We have not actually retired, although the Colonel is now in his eighties. His commitment to do publicity for the Kentucky Fried Chicken Corporation and to make commercials for television and radio keep him very busy. Then, too, there is his Kentucky Fried Chicken franchise business in Canada which operates as a charity and occupies a great deal of his time.

"Then, too, I have a connection with the Marion-Kay Company of Brownstown, Indiana. This company puts out a chicken seasoning under my name and with my picture on the packages. I do not think there are better spices to be found anywhere than Marion-Kay spices. We use them in our restaurants and I am kept busy promoting them and recommending them to all my friends."

-9-

It is surprising to learn that people like the Colonel or Claudia, whose lives have been centered around fried chicken and other delicious items of food, would have for their diet for days on end nothing but rice and fruit. But this is exactly the diet the Colonel and Claudia subsisted on for weeks during several periods of their lives. Both are active and vigorous and it is essential that they feel well at all times. So, whenever their weights climbed beyond a certain level and they felt sluggish they knew it was time to take the situation in hand.

It all started one day when the Colonel said to Claudia, "I think we would both feel better if we lost some pounds. I heard of a clinic in Durham, North Carolina, which puts you on a health diet and watches you while you lose weight. Let's try it and see if we both don't feel better."

Claudia agreed. A few days later they found themselves in Durham and entered the clinic.

"No one enjoys feeling like a guinea pig," says Claudia, "especially the Colonel who doesn't want people fooling with him. But we suffered the ordeal of the initial physical examination the doctor in charge of the clinic gave us for we knew it was all for our own good."

The clinic itself was a pleasant place. The building was light and airy and the surroundings more or less cheerful and not too much like a hospital. But doctors' offices are doctors' offices and there is always the familiar odor of medicine to identify them as such.

"Even though you are not sick," says Claudia, "whenever a doctor examines you, you look for the worst and wonder what he will find wrong with you."

But in the cases of Claudia and the Colonel their examinations did not disclose any disorders and the doctor ended up by saying to them, "So. You came here to lose weight? Well, if you do exactly as we tell you and follow our instructions, we'll not only get your weight down but we will make you feel like new people when you leave here."

"Humph!" grunted the Colonel. "I don't want to feel like someone else. I'm satisfied to be what I am. Just help me to feel better and nothing else. Besides, I like Claudia the way she is, too," he added with a laugh.

The doctor laughed at the Colonel's banter and assured him he would not make new people out of him and Claudia.

"Some people need to be made over, but not you," he quipped.

After finishing his examination and getting the results of the various tests he had given them, the doctor issued his instructions, which he insisted they were to follow to the letter. He told them he was prescribing a diet for each of them and that it was being sent to the kitchen and would be served to them regularly in the dining room of the Diet House. He also instructed them to take daily walks.

Claudia tells us, "We were able to live in a hotel in Durham but had to return to the clinic for our three meals each day and for a daily checkup the doctor gave each person who attended the clinic. The doctor told us how much weight he wanted us to lose and just how fast, or I should say how slowly, we were to lose it. We have visited this clinic three or four times during the past fifteen years and found each stay to be most beneficial to our health and well-being.

"On each occasion we were there, the clinic put us on what it called its 'rice diet'. For breakfast we were served one-half grapefruit with no sugar and were allowed to drink one cup of tea or decaffeinated coffee without cream or sugar. It was at lunch and dinner we were given the rice. It came to the table steamed and unseasoned. With it was a small serving of either fresh fruit or fruit that had been canned in light syrup. At these two meals we were allowed one cup of tea or decaffeinated coffee, but no cream or sugar. Believe you me! After five or six weeks of this diet of steamed rice anything white began to look unpleasant. But I have to say it was worth it, for when we finished our course, as you might call it, we left the clinic feeling lighter, not only in weight, but in spirits as well.

"On one occasion," and Claudia laughs as she speaks, "when we entered the clinic we were able to rent a furnished apartment which, unfortunately for us, had a well equipped kitchen. Well, between the subtle lure of this kitchen and the steady diet of rice, we succumbed one evening to temptation and fixed ourselves a good meal after we had eaten the rice dinner at the diet house.

"The next day when we took our daily physical checkup the doctor, after taking our blood pressure and going through his routine, put his stethoscope on his desk and looked at us severely.

"You cheated!" he said, bluntly. "And don't think we can't tell it either!"

"Then, in mock anger, he dressed us down and told us we would not get the full benefit of our stay at the clinic if we did not follow his orders to the letter.

"When we left his office, the Colonel said to me, 'I feel like a little boy who has been kept after school by his teacher'. I knew just what he meant for I felt the same way.

"After that unhappy experience," Claudia chuckles, "we did no more cheating on our diet and each time we visited the clinic we came away feeling we could lick the world."

But the Colonel and Claudia would leave the clinic only to return to the routine of travelling and advertising the Kentucky Fried Chicken by the personal appearances the Colonel made. This, naturally, meant attending banquets and luncheons at which delicious and fattening foods were served. The result was that after a few years of this the Colonel would look at Claudia and say, "Honey, I'm beginning to feel sluggish. My weight is up again and I can see you are filling out your clothes more than is good for you. I think it is time for us to head for Durham."

"So. There we would be again," laughs Claudia, "looking at the rice and dreaming of fried chicken."

Although not what one would call a health buff, the Colonel is one to look out for himself and see that Claudia, too, keeps herself

CLAUDIA

physically fit. He will take advantage of every opportunity to give himself physical tone and, on one occasion while visiting western Canada, he suggested to Claudia that they spend some time at a health spa which featured warm mineral water baths.

Claudia tells us that the water was furnished by hot springs which formed large pools. These pools had been walled in and one could stand in them and even walk around or swim a little while getting the relaxing and salutary effects of the warm water.

"At one particular spa," Claudia tells us, smiling as she talks, "a joke was played on another woman and me. After spending our allotted time in the water we would go into a waiting room to rest and cool off. There were two of these rooms, one for the men and another for the women, and from each there was a door leading into a room where you could get a rubdown. Some pranksters seeing that this other woman and I were most modest and proper persons, wanted to have some fun with us. They extolled the virtues of these rubdowns and told us we must not fail to have one. What they did not tell us, however, was that the persons who gave the massages were two young Swedish men! So, we walked blandly and innocently into the massage room expecting to be greeted by a masseuse, not a masseur! Imagine our surprise on coming face to face with two men! Not knowing what to do and being quite disturbed, but at the same time wanting to save face, we held tightly onto the sheets wrapped around us and were given a very proper and modest rubdown. When we came out of the massage room and back into the room where the pranksters were sitting we kept straight faces and acted as if this were something we did all the time. When the pranksters asked us questions about our experience we acted wise and blasé. We smiled as enigmatically as we could and raised our eyebrows and shrugged our shoulders slightly, but said nothing. I think this plagued our pranksters and in the end I believe we had the most fun out of the little joke."

When the Colonel expanded his franchise business into Canada it meant spending a great deal of time in that country and in travelling to many parts of it. By this time the business had grown to such an extent that Claudia no longer had to prepare the recipe herself as this was now done by members of a large staff of employees. Claudia now acted alongside her husband in the role of executive. This meant she could travel with the Colonel anytime she wished, and she took advantage of every opportunity to accompany him. The two of them learned to love Canada and its people. They became especially fond of the scenery of western Canada and spent one summer driving from Ontario to Alberta, staying for some time in Banff and Jasper.

Claudia waxes most enthusiastic in talking about this trip and in telling about Lake Louise and the mountains. "They make up some of the most beautiful scenery I have ever seen," she will tell you. "The whole experience of being in that country is exciting," she says. "And one of the most thrilling things we did was to take a snowmobile ride out onto the ice field. These snowmobiles are large ones and have a circular seat enclosed by a glass dome so that you can look out onto the ice without getting too cold from the breeze. It's a thrilling experience. The guides who take parties out on the ride do not go slowly but really drive at a fast clip. And the bouncing! This bouncing is the one thing I guess everyone who takes the ride will never forget! It certainly adds to the thrill and the excitement. But, for me at least, it took away a little of the enjoyment I would have had of the view of the mountains in the distance. Although, at that, I had fun and today can look back on all the bouncing with a laugh."

Another feature of this trip that thrilled Claudia was being able to watch the wild animals of the area.

"They have become used to people," she says, "and some of them seem almost tame, especially the bears which come close to the hotels and rob the garbage cans.

"There is one hotel I remember with great pleasure," she goes on to say. "It has a large dining room with huge picture windows so that you can sit at your table and while you eat look out on the mountains with their snow-covered peaks. Often, just outisde these windows bears would appear and search for food. They were a delight to watch and it was a special treat for the diners if a mother bear showed up with her cubs. There would usually be two small bears with a mother bear and they would play and cavort like a couple of kittens. No floor show in any night club could rival them for the fun and entertainment they gave the guests on these occasions. It reminded me a great deal of watching the bears in the Great Smoky Mountains, and I never tired of looking at them.

"But like bears everywhere these bears can be dangerous, and one should never be foolish enough to get too close to them or let them take food from one's hand.

"Besides being dangerous, at times these bears were just plain mischievous and could make a nuisance of themselves. One family told us they had spread out their picnic cloth on which they had put their appetizing lunch and were waiting to eat as soon as some steaks they were cooking over an open fire were done, when a bear appeared and invited himself to the feast. All the members of this hapless family rushed to their car, locked themselves in, and watched helplessly as the bear indulged himself, eating not only the lunch on the cloth, but the hot steaks as well which he raked away from the fire and, hot as they were, downed them with gusto!

"They told me," says Claudia, "that they were mighty hungry and angry when they returned to their hotel that evening, but that now they can look back on the experience and laugh about it.

"I could tell," Claudia adds with a chuckle," that they had reached the stage where they enjoyed telling the story and I imagine the bear gets bigger and the steaks hotter with each telling."

-10-

After establishing his franchises in Canada the Colonel found he had to make many trips to the Canadian Home Office which was located in Toronto. Many times these trips from Kentucky were made by automobile with the Colonel and Claudia dividing the driving between them. But more often they flew for the convenience and speed that air travel offered.

"Some years before we began all this air travel we are doing today," Claudia says, "I realized I would have to make many flights if I wanted to keep up with the Colonel. Before that time, I had never been in a plane and did not know if I would like flying. Like many people, I had heard and read stories about plane crashes, and some of my friends who were afraid to fly were always telling me about the dangers of air travel. So, one day just for the experience I flew from Asheville, North Carolina, to Knoxville, Tennessee. I will never forget that flight. I was somewhat nervous getting on the plane and taking my seat by the window. I don't know if the stewardess was aware of how apprehensive I was for I was trying to act as though I had been flying all my life. But anyway, she was very attentive and her manner put me at ease. I felt fairly comfortable until we were told to fasten our seat belts. I knew this meant the plane was getting ready to take off and that my moment of truth had come. I felt very important fastening my seat belt for the first time and I think this helped give me a feeling of confidence. I settled back in my seat and looked out the window. The plane started to move slowly and continued at a rather slow speed for some time. This disturbed me, for I thought to myself, 'We will never get off the ground at this speed. We are bound to crash'. But then I learned we were only taxiing to the runway from which the plane would take off. When we reached this runway the plane made a sharp right turn without stopping and began to pick up speed. It was very thrilling and, far from being scared, I was fascinated and have been so ever since whenever I am a passenger on a plane. I like the roar and the speed and the feeling of power of the big motors. Every time we fly, it is the same exhilerating experience for me and I do not think I will ever tire of it."

Sometime later, Claudia took her second flight. This time it was with the Colonel on a pleasure trip to Los Angeles. At least, it was a pleasure trip for Claudia. For the Colonel, it was business as usual.

"For the Colonel, every trip is a business trip," says Claudia. "But he enjoys them as much as if they were for pleasure only. In fact, we no longer plan a vacation. We really have a year-long vacation as our work is so agreeable."

But they do get tired and there are times Claudia and the Colonel like to stay at home in their beautiful house in Kentucky. After living for several years in the subdivision near Louisville, the Colonel began to yearn for country life. He wanted a place where he could stretch his legs and have a garden in the peace and quiet of the country.

The Colonel was in the habit of driving to Shelbyville to get his hair cut by his favorite barber. One day while in the barber's chair he casually remarked that he would like to buy a small farm and asked the barber to let him know if he heard of anything being available. His barber told him that just that morning another customer had told him he would like to sell a thirty-two acre tract on which he had just built a modern dwelling. On hearing this the Colonel asked where the land was located and learning it was on a paved road just a few miles north of Shelbyville hurried out to see it. He liked what he saw and made a deal with the owner on the spot.

Claudia tells us, "As soon as he closed the deal, the Colonel became very impatient to move into the house and decided not to wait until he had sold his house near Louisville to do so.

The residence of Colonel and Mrs. Harland Sanders is located near Shelbyville, Kentucky, and is one of her "dream houses with electricity."

CLAUDIA

"Since it seems very hard to say 'no' to the Colonel the former owners of the small farm suddenly saw two house guests they didn't expect descend on them in the form of the Colonel and me. The Colonel just moved right in on them! Everyone took this good-naturedly but I am sure it must have been a trial to that poor couple and their two teenage children. The Colonel had our piano put in their living room and one of our beds into the bedroom next to the other couple's bed and a dresser put beside their dresser. He stored our box spring mattresses by standing them on end along the walls of several rooms and put other pieces of furniture throughout the house until the place looked like an overcrowded furniture store. In fact you could hardly see the floor and I wonder to this day how any of us got around that house. We slept in the lower level in what you might call a huge utility room. Fortunately, we were like one big happy family living all over the house so that the arrangement was not quite as bad as it sounds.

"We lived like this for several months while the other family built a house on two adjoining acres the Colonel sold them."

It was during this time that the Colonel set out twenty-seven trees since the little farm had only one tree on it when he bought it. Impatient again, the Colonel did not want to wait for trees to grow so the ones he set out were quite tall, some of them forty feet or more in height.

"All in all, we enjoyed those few hectic months and while I am sure it must have been a trying time for the other family we can all look back on it now and have a good laugh," Claudia says.

She goes on, "We call our house near Shelbyville our home. But we are away from it so much that it is almost like one of the places we visit. We also have a house in Canada and it is another home to us."

Visiting Canada as often as his business required him to do convinced the Colonel that he should have permanent living quarters there. So the little girl who played with the pebble houses and wondered if she would ever have a house with electricity found herself the mistress of two lovely modern dwellings.

"We bought a three-bedroom, tri-level, brick dwelling on the outskirts of Toronto. I like the place so well that I often go there without the Colonel. My daughter, Billie Jean and I drive there and spend happy weeks at a time in a carefree vacation. The weather is to my liking and I find it especially pleasant in the summertime.

"Then there are times I like to diet to lose a little weight without going to the diet clinic in North Carolina, and for some reason I find I can do this more easily in our northern home than in Kentucky. The Canadian subdivision we live in is a quiet one and Billie Jean and I can take long walks in the evening to work off a few pounds. The only trouble we have ever had has been with dogs. But you find dogs in every subdivision. After a while we learned where the unfriendly dogs were and avoided those areas.

"When we first bought our home in Canada," Claudia goes on, "we felt safer there than we did in Kentucky. Crime had not yet reached that part of Canada to a great extent. But I am sorry to say that as the population around Toronto grew and many outsiders began coming into the area, crime and vice increased there as it has everywhere. Thankfully, the neighborhood our house is located in has remained stable, and we still feel safe and take our evening walks even if the dogs do get after us once in a while."

But going to and from their homes in Canada and Kentucky is to the Colonel and Claudia what commuting to the office is to the average person. Today, their travels are worldwide and it is nothing for them to make trips to Europe, Africa, South America, or the Far East.

Prior to the time the Colonel developed his franchise business into a worldwide operation, the trips he and Claudia took were either pleasure trips or short business trips in the United States. But with the phenomenal growth of the Kentucky Fried Chicken business and its subsequent sale the Colonel found himself travelling, not only throughout the United States, but to all parts of the world as well.

If it is true that travelling is like getting a college education both the Colonel and Claudia should rank with the PhDs. Over the past twenty-odd years their travels have taken them to all fifty states of

CLAUDIA

the United States and to more than thirty countries.

"Our shoes have touched the soil of every continent," says Claudia. And she can go on from there to discuss intelligently and knowledgeably country after country which she has visited. As if following Lord Chesterfield's advice to his son, Claudia saw what she looked at, asked questions, and learned. Her mind, like her camera, caught and retained her experiences.

"I have only one regret about my travels," she will tell you. "And that is that so many of the places we visited are today much like the United States. The buildings are familiar looking, and the clothes the people wear are so much like those you see at home that it is sometimes difficult to realize you are in a foreign country.

"I was especially thrilled in the Orient," she goes on. "There, most of the people dressed in what you would call native costumes and the distinctive architecture is very unlike that of our Western civilization. I get what to me is a pleasant feeling of being far away when I see signs in Arabic or in the Japanese or Chinese characters. This has always been a real thrill to me, although I have sadly noticed that many of our North American customs and modes of dress are beginning to infiltrate even Asia and many remote parts of the earth. But I guess I shouldn't complain for, after all, are we not trying to get the peoples of the world to eat Kentucky Fried chicken?" This she says with a laugh.

For both the pleasure and the educational value afforded by travel the Colonel and Claudia often take side trips, using as bases the countries the Colonel visits to make television commercials.

One year the Colonel made commercials in Spain, and this gave them the opportunity to visit Portugal and even to cross the Mediterranean into North Africa for a jaunt to Casablanca. From Spain their business took them to England to make more commercials and the two of them arranged to go by way of Switzerland to spend a few days in that delightful country.

"When you are away from home, it is very easy to tell yourself, 'Oh. I will get back here again some day'. But this is a mistake and the time to see what you want to see is when you are there and not to put it off for some future visit which may never materialize," observes Claudia, philosophically. "That is why we take these little side trips and see as much as we can whenever we are away from home. But sometimes we do get back, and then we have the pleasure of revisiting just that many more places. The Colonel has returned more often than I to many of the foreign places he has visited. He has been to Australia three times and I do not know how many times to England and other countries of Europe.

"Our business trips are somewhat different from those of the average business person. We are always attending banquets and the Colonel is always involved in making public appearances. So, you see, we welcome every opportunity to get away by ourselves and enjoy some parts of our trips as anonymous tourists. This is often hard to do for the Colonel is recognized everywhere and we are seldom allowed much time just to ourselves."

Due to sensible and careful eating habits, the Colonel and Claudia have never been ill on any of their trips. They are careful to drink only bottled water and not to eat foods such as lettuce which might have been rinsed in native tap water.

"We even brush our teeth using bottled water," explains Claudia. "I even went so far one time as to turn down soft drinks when I saw the bottles were being kept cold by being submerged in ice water. Many members of the groups we travelled with got very sick at times, but the Colonel and I managed to stay well by taking a few simple precautions. We eat only fruit we can peel. We drink, besides bottled water, only coffee or tea which has been boiled. I am also careful about the meat I eat. One day, in Egypt, a huge platter of what looked like the roasted lower leg of some large animal was placed on our table. I really didn't know what it was, but it looked suspiciously like the leg of a camel and I wasn't about to take any chances. I refused to eat any of it.

"We were often served goat meat which I am able to eat, although it is not what I would call my favorite dish. I remember being served a great deal of it in Jamaica, especially curried goat meat which seems to be a great favorite of the people there. The Colonel had to go to Jamaica one year on a promotion trip for the Kentucky Fried Chicken Company and I went along just for the fun of it. I had a great time there and made one of my rare visits to the race track. I discovered I could put up dollar bets on the horses and it reminded me of the days during the depression in the United States when many race tracks reduced the betting from a two-dollar ticket to a one dollar ticket."

When asked if she won or lost that day, Claudia smiled enigmatically and replied, "That is my little secret."

While in the Caribbean she and the Colonel visited Puerto Rico and as usual took advantage of the opportunity to tour the island and learn what they could about its history, its people, and its commerce.

"The coffee plantations are what fascinated me the most on that island," asserts Claudia with enthusiasm. "We rented a car with a driver and he took us into what you might call the back country to see them. He explained many things to us, not only about the coffee plantations, but about the island in general. While I was aware that sugar processing was the main industry I was surprised to learn that a great deal of tobacco is grown there and this made me think of my home state of Kentucky. From the number of people we saw on this small island, especially in the cities, I told the Colonel I thought children must be the main crop. I did learn later that Puerto Rico has one of the highest population densities in the world. This crowded condition, coupled with the fact that the economy of Puerto Rico was based mainly on its sugar crop, had caused the island to suffer economically. But with the addition of a variety of other crops now produced commercially and with modern know-how I hope to see a continued improvement in the standard of living for the people of this beautiful island.

"From one of the coffee plantations we visited I brought back a small branch from a coffee tree which, besides its leaves, also had some coffee beans in various stages of becoming ripe. Some were red and some were green. In all, I thought it would make a beautiful memento of my trip and on returning home I took it to a shop to have it preserved and framed. But, unfortunately, before this could be done the branch dried out and the leaves and beans fell off. So I just had to forget about it. But whenever I drink a cup of coffee today I am reminded of my visit to the coffee plantations of Puerto Rico and the coffee tastes just a little better and my life is the richer for it."

Claudia goes on. "As you know, the Colonel is one who is always mixing pleasure with business and managing to do it successfully every time in spite of the age-old motto against this mixture. That is, almost every time," she adds with a laugh. "For there was the time we went to Russia. We went there with a religious group, and were supposed to be taking a pleasure trip only, to learn about the USSR by visiting it personally and seeing it for ourselves.

"Well, you know the Colonel," Claudia was referring to the day they packed to go on this trip to the Soviet Union and she had come upon the Colonel putting a large pressure cooker into a cardboard box and placing it with his luggage.

"What on earth are you going to do with that? Cook our meals on this trip?" she exclaimed.

"I'm going to take it with me," the Colonel responded. "There is bound to be someone among the millions of Russians who will be interested in learning how to cook Kentucky Fried Chicken."

"But there is no free enterprise in Russia," Claudia told him.

"I know that," the Colonel retorted. "But I still think someone will be interested and I won't be satisfied until I find out."

"Well," returned Claudia. "I don't think the Russians will be interested. The only American chicken they would be interested in would be a Rhode Island Red."

"Oh, go on with you," snorted the Colonel. And he went on packing his pressure cooker with the same enthusiasm he showed when he prepared to visit a prospective franchisee in the next state.

When they got to Moscow the Colonel did everything in his power to find someone who would let him show how to cook chicken. His efforts were all in vain as no Russian would dare display interest in anything even remotely related to capitalism. This was one time

CLAUDIA

Claudia had been right. The Colonel finally gave up and repacked his pressure cooker in its cardboard box.

"He ended up by giving the cooker to our guide in Jerusalem," Claudia informs us with a chuckle.

"I had heard many stories of women working in Russia," Claudia says. "But I am used to seeing women working in the United States. I have seen women police officers and women taxi drivers and I remember well the women of my childhood who worked in the fields with their husbands on their farms much like the pioneer women who helped develop our country. In the cities of Russia I saw women cleaning the streets and in the country I saw them laboring in the fields. I did not see many young men doing jobs of this kind, although I saw many men in uniform and watched them drill under what I imagine were closely guarded occasions for the benefit of the tourists. Perhaps most of the able-bodied young men were in the army and this left the laboring jobs to the women. It rather reminded me of the years of World War II when women did many of the tasks we usually think of as being performed by men.

"The guide on this trip was a woman and a very interesting person she was. Her English was flawless and she spoke without the least accent. She told our group that she had been trained by the government for her work as a tourist guide and that she had made the choice early in life. Her education was accordingly designed to fit her for this occupation which was to be her life's work and her contribution to Communism. 'You choose what you want to be,' she told us, 'and if you are qualified the government will train you for it. This is all free to the people. There is no limit to how high a position a person can attain if one is able. There is no limit to what Communism can do for you if you have the ability or are talented. And it is all free.'

"Of course, we know it is not free," observes Claudia. "In the Russians' case it might not cost money. But to Americans the price is the loss of freedom, and we consider that our most priceless possession.

"The lady guide was very affable and answered most of our questions with candor. It was only when she was asked specific questions about Communism or questions bordering on State secrets that she would cleverly parry them and sometimes would avoid answering them at all by adroitly changing the subject.

"One of the ministers in our group asked the guide about religion in Russia. The little lady gave him what she intended to be a tolerant smile and politely told him that, to her, religion was a fairy tale and that she did not believe in God. Personally, I can't help but feel that somewhere deep inside she had doubts as she said this, although I may be wrong. It is said we believe what we are taught to believe when we are very young. This may be true, but I don't think it is entirely true, for we often see great thinkers breaking with the traditions they were taught in their childhood. I guess this makes for progress," she observes. "But sometimes I have seen a man's thinking tend to set the world backwards.

"Moscow is an interesting city," Claudia goes on. "The public buildings are imposing and the monuments impressive. Emphasis is mainly on the functional side of life. There is some accent on the aesthetic, but not to the noticeable extent we found it in other countries we visited. Russia has its ballet and its music, but to me it all seems state oriented and designed to teach the Russian version of Communism."

Russia was not the only Communist country Claudia and the Colonel visited. They spent some time in Germany and while in Berlin took a bus tour of East Berlin, passing through Checkpoint Charlie to get into the Russian section of the city. When the bus stopped at the checkpoint a Russian guide boarded it to take the place of the West Berlin guide who had accompanied the bus as far as the Berlin Wall. The guide from East Berlin, like the guide in Moscow, was also a woman.

"The Russians are very strict and meticulous about checking up on visitors," says Claudia. "A Russian soldier got on the bus with the Russian guide and looked over the papers of each passenger. He walked slowly down the aisle gradually making his way to the back of the bus all the while taking each passenger's passport and examining it carefully before handing it back. He did all this without saying a word, or smiling. When he came to one of the ladies in our party he seemed to become disturbed. We were all members of the National Restaurant Association and the lady who seemed to upset the soldier was a very respectable individual. The soldier kept looking at her passport and then at her. Finally, he said, 'Take off your glasses'. The little lady complied and we all watched as the soldier continued to stare at her and look at her passport. Then, without a word, he handed the passport back to her and went on to the next passenger. Finished with the last member of our group, the soldier got off the bus saying something in Russian as he passed the guide on his way back down the aisle to the front door. She, in turn, told our driver he could proceed as soon as the soldier got off the bus. We later learned that the federal case the soldier had made about the lady's passport was due to the fact that she was not wearing glasses when she had had her passport picture taken. It was only when the soldier saw her after she had removed her glasses that he was satisfied she was the person pictured on her passport. The lady took it goodnaturedly, saying it would be an experience she would always remember. But she did add somewhat disgustedly that at all the borders she had crossed no other official had raised the question about her picture.

"Of course," Claudia goes on, "we were shown only what the Russians wanted us to see in East Berlin. Our guide spoke excellent English and she used her extensive vocabularly to great advantage in pointing out the sights to us in glowing terms.

"The only time we were permitted to get off the bus was when it stopped at the various monuments erected in memory of the Russians killed in World War II. What annoyed all of us was the fact that all the guide talked about was what Russia had done in the war and the numbers of Russians who lost their lives. You would think from the way she talked that no other country had lost any men or had done anything toward winning the War. But they still liked our U.S. money. At these monuments there were souvenir stands operated by the government. I bought some postcards and offered to pay for them with Canadian coins I happened to have in my purse. But the man in charge of the booth refused to accept them and insisted I pay with United States money."

Claudia had quite an experience while she was in West Berlin. A West German restaurant group took the American group to the West Berlin Airport for luncheon in the airport's second floor dining room. This dining room was large and light and airy. Huge picture windows afforded a beautiful view of the airstrips and, as the party ate, they could watch the planes land and take off. After finishing luncheon the group walked downstairs to the bus which was to take the members back to their hotel.

Claudia tells us, "On the way out, I stopped at the ladies' room and when I came out and walked to the front of the airport building I saw my bus pull off and leave without me.

" 'Well,' I thought to myself, 'they will miss me and come back'.

"So, I found a comfortable chair and sat down to wait. I waited and I waited. But no bus.

" 'Humph,' I said under my breath. 'I guess I don't rate so high, after all. They haven't missed me.'

"I didn't panic. I just looked around until I found a cab driver who spoke English. I told him my story and gave him the name of my hotel. When we arrived there I found that the members of my group had finally missed me and were beginning to get worried. They were relieved when they saw me and besieged me with questions, most of all asking if I hadn't been frightened. They could not believe I was as calm as I appeared and that getting 'lost', as they put it, hadn't alarmed me.

"The Colonel later asked me if I had had any trouble finding someone who spoke English. I told him 'No', that nearly everyone in the countries we visited spoke English.

" 'I wonder why that is', he said.

" 'Because they want our money', I told him."

-11-

Although Claudia was kept busy overseeing the operation of her restaurant, The Claudia Sanders Dinner House, which she had opened near Shelbyville, Kentucky in 1968, she still found time to travel both for pleasure and on business trips with the Colonel.

Over the years, she and the Colonel had visited so many countries that a list of them would read like a moderate gazetteer. This list would include Australia, Canada, Denmark, Egypt, England, Finland, France, Germany, Israel, Japan, Morocco, Norway, Portugal, Russia, Spain, and Sweden, to name some of these countries. And this does not include the countries of South America nor the many cities and places of note they visited on their travels.

"We enjoyed our stay in Japan very much," says Claudia. "The Colonel went there to promote the Kentucky Fried Chicken franchises in that country. We spent some time in Tokyo and Osaka and in both large cities were regally entertained by the Japanese business men who operated the Kentucky Fried Chicken franchises. Language was no problem as these men spoke perfect English.

"We did not go to Hiroshima nor to Nagasaki which were the targets for the atom bombs dropped on Japan in August of 1945. I was just as glad not to see these cities for, to me, they are tragic landmarks in a sad chapter of mankind's bloody history.

"But I was thrilled," she goes on, "flying over Fujiyama. The cone-like symmetry of this extinct volcano is so beautiful it is breathtaking. The summit is snow-capped and the crater is circular. It has been a sacred mountain since ancient times and until 1868 no woman was ever permitted to climb it. I had to laugh to myself. Here in the modern days of women's liberation I was even higher than its summit and I thought to myself that the old *shoguns* would turn over in their graves if they knew that feminine eyes were looking down at, and not up to, their sacred mountain.

"I was surprised to see how modern Japan is. It is hard to believe that feudalism was abolished only a little over a hundred years ago and that 1868 marks the beginning of the Meiji reforms which began the industrialization of the islands. I do not think that Commodore Perry nor the Japanese leaders could have foreseen the great changes that were to take place in the way of life of the Japanese peoples when they negotiated the treaty that first opened Japan to the ships of the United States. And to think that all this finally led to Kentucky Fried Chicken in Japan," she adds with her customary chuckle.

Some of Claudia's trips gave her soul-satisfying experiences and others gave her more worldly thrills. In referring to her trip to the Holy Land with the Colonel, Claudia tells us this visit gave her both kinds of these experiences. The first was being baptized with the Colonel in the Jordan River; the other was the bus ride through no-man's-land.

At the time of her visit to the Holy Land, relations between the Arabs and the Israelis were strained almost to the breaking point and no one would have been too surprised if all-out war had broken out. Efforts were made to keep the two antagonists from getting at each other's throats. Among the steps taken was the creation of a no-man's-land through which traffic was allowed to pass only during certain hours of the day and all unauthorized vehicles had to be out of the area by five o'clock in the evening.

"I knew this," Claudia informs us. "So, as we rode back to our hotel after a day of sightseeing, I kept looking at my watch and wishing the driver would speed up a little, although I had no idea of how far we had to go to get out of the area. I also noticed that the driver kept looking out both sides of the bus, scrutinizing the hilltops as we passed them. I had read about the advantage the possession of the high ground gave troops so I figured our guide was looking for

CLAUDIA

trouble to come from that direction if it came at all. After a while I found myself watching the hilltops, too. I did not say anything to the Colonel about my feelings of apprehension. But I don't think it would have bothered him. He probably would have snorted and said something like 'Let them start something. We'll finish it'.

"On both sides of the road," Claudia goes on, "were tanks and soldiers with guns. It was like being in a war and it was rather scary. I assured myself I was in no danger since I had been baptized in the Jordan River. But I also found great comfort in looking at the two machine guns on the floor near the driver's seat and within easy reach of that individual. I don't know if the driver had been baptized, or not, but I could see that he was well aware of the old adage that the Lord helps those who help themselves."

Fortunately for Claudia, that day the bus ride was without incident and all her thrills were in her imagination. But this day on the bus was an unusual one and the other days of her trips were the normal days of a world traveller. They were pleasureable and enjoyable, without the element of danger of that memorable day in Israel.

Back about the time the Colonel was beginning to franchise his Kentucky Fried Chicken business, he made a trip to Australia to attend a church convention in hopes of finding help to stop the "cussin" to which he had become addicted in the early, trying years of his hard life.

"The Colonel fell in love with Australia," Claudia informs us. "He was very eager to return, taking me with him. We did not get there for several years after the Colonel's first visit, but when we did I, too, fell in love, not only with Australia, but with Polynesia as well."

Claudia remembers one experience she had in Australia with great pleasure. It was being in a commercial the Colonel made for the Kentucky Fried Chicken Company which by now had found its way "down under".

I didn't do much in this commercial," Claudia says with a laugh. "I just sat at a table with some other folks and was served fried chicken—Kentucky Fried Chicken, of course. One thing I'll say is that I didn't have to be a professional actress to show I liked it. All I had to do was take a bite and my expression did the rest."

One year, Claudia and the Colonel took a trip to New Zealand to spend time on both the North and South Islands.

"I was again surprised," states Claudia "to find modern civilization in what I had always envisioned as a faraway place. I guess the strange sounding names give us this impression. This shows the value of travel. There is no substitute for going somewhere to see other lands for yourself.

"I have met people who live in these faraway places who, when I tell them I am from Kentucky, look at me rather strangely and I can almost read their minds. I am sure they are thinking I must come from some wild part of the world where all the men wear coonskin caps and carry long rifles."

The trip to New Zealand was a holiday spree for Claudia and the Colonel. There were no business worries on their minds; just the desire to see the sights and enjoy themselves. Of course, as soon as the plane landed the Colonel headed straightway to an orphanage to see the "kiddies". He loves children with the genuine affection of a kindly and tender grandfather. It is said that it is more blessed to give than to receive, but of all giving, the giving not of things, but of one's self, is by far the greatest. And the Colonel does this fully and without affectation. Claudia possesses this quality also, but in a more reserved and less demonstrative fashion.

"I let the Colonel do the performing," she smiles. "Everything he does, whether it is for business or to make little children happy, he does so gracefully and so well. Anything I might do would only be an anticlimax."

And therein lies Claudia's tremendous value and her priceless contribution to their partnership. When the Colonel is on the scene anything attempted by someone else would only suffer by comparison.

"After bringing some joy to the little ones at the orphanage," Claudia says, "the Colonel put his efforts into seeing that we enjoyed our stay in New Zealand. He escorted me over both the large islands in such an urbane manner that I was reminded again of Aunt

Elizabeth and her stories of the White Knight who would come into my life.

"I find that so many places in the world which are far apart have much in common," observes Claudia. "For instance, in Rotorua the thermal baths reminded me of the warm springs in Canada. Looking at Mount Cook and the Tasman Glacier transported me in memory to the Alps of Europe and the Rocky Mountains of the Western United States and Canada.

"How alike, and yet so different, are the places of this world," she says philosophically.

"We saw some of the native Maoris of New Zealand, and I thought of our American Indians and how both these free peoples had been conquered by the white man and their lands taken from them. In our search for knowledge, the Colonel and I visited a museum devoted to the history and the culture of the Maori people and learned much about their way of life, both historically and how they now are adjusting to the coming of Western Civilization to their part of the world. They were a fierce people and resisted many attempts to subdue them. But today many of them, like many of our American Indians, have accepted the ways of the white man and are fitting themselves into the modern customs of civilization. Again we see some of the colorful past disappearing into the realm of history.

"I enjoyed the mountain climbing we did to see Mount Cook and the Tasman Glacier," Claudia says with a sly smile. "We did it by ski-plane," she clarifies. "We took off from the Mount Cook Airport and climbed past rugged icefalls and snow-covered slopes. Finally, the eighteen-mile long Tasman Glacier came into view. The pilot lowered the retractable skis and we landed on a vast snowfield at an elevation of some seven thousand feet. This was truly mountaineering in an armchair!"

Today, although time adds years to the aging of their bodies, Claudia and the Colonel remain as young in spirit as they ever were.

"Never look over your shoulder," she will advise you. "Always look forward to a goal. This will keep you from giving up and it will keep you young."

Claudia follows her own good advice. She keeps looking forward and finds that delightful things are still happening for her. In 1973 she was not only presented with an honorary degree of Doctor of Laws from Union College of Barbourville, Kentucky, but she was also made a Kentucky Colonel.

"I am very proud to be a Kentucky Colonel," she says. "Although I never feature it nor refer to myself as Colonel Claudia. I think one Colonel in the family is enough," she laughs.

Today, at an age at which most persons have retired, Claudia finds herself launched on new activities. She is following the Colonel's

Claudia in her Cap and Gown after receiving her Doctor of Laws degree at Union College, in Barbourville, Ky. 'in recognition of notable achievement in the field of business, outstanding leadership in civic affairs and distinguished service to higher education.' This was on August 15, 1974

example and is franchising her restaurants under the name of Claudia Sanders Dinner House. As we have seen, she opened the the first restaurant in 1968 near Shelbyville, Kentucky, and operated it herself for several years before franchising it to Thomas and Cherry Settle who have the distinction of being her first franchisees.

Also following in the Colonel's footsteps she made her second commercial, this time for the restaurant near Shelbyville. The commercial, which was first shown on television on April 17, 1975, consists of two parts. One shows her standing in front of the restaurant. In the other she is shown standing inside the building in one of the dining rooms. In both segments she has a speaking part and invites the public to come to the Dinner House to enjoy one of its delicious meals.

In October 1975, the second Claudia Sanders Dinner House was opened. It is located near Bowling Green, Kentucky, and, like the restaurant near Shelbyville, it also follows the Southern tradition. It is housed in a pre-Civil War mansion which sits high on a hill and is shaded by beautiful, large trees.

"We are very pleased with the ante-bellum atmosphere of this location. It is a fitting setting for our delicious food," Claudia observes.

To get the restaurant started successfully, Jim Sanders was called upon to help in Bowling Green as he had done in Shelbyville where he worked for some six months training the kitchen staff. Jim Sanders is a nephew of the Colonel and with his mustache and goatee bears a striking resemblance to his famous uncle. Not only does he look like the Colonel, but his skill in the kitchen ranks second only to that of the Colonel himself.

Claudia tells us, "Jim is a highly skilled chef who can cook any of the dishes served by the Claudia Sanders Dinner Houses. Not only can he prepare the main courses of meats and vegetables but he can make salads, bake pies and cakes, and prepare all kinds of desserts and other delicacies. He has been indispensable to us. Like the Colonel, he is a hard and willing worker who is constantly seeking more knowledge of the culinary art."

Perhaps, during the years she has spent with the Colonel, some of his vigor and enthusiasm have been catching for Claudia is not satisfied just to franchise her restaurants, but to get into another activity as well. She has set out upon a new venture—the nation-wide sale of old country hams under the name of Claudia Sanders Kentucky Country Hams.

"I think," she declares, "that there is no ham better than properly cured and aged old country ham and no old country ham better than Kentucky old country ham.

"We have developed a process of curing and aging ham that gives the meat a distinctive and unusual flavor. After seeing how well the public received our hams in the Shelbyville restaurant we felt we should sell them nation-wide as well as supply them to all the Claudia Sanders Dinner Houses."

Fred Settle, Jr., a brother of Thomas Settle, had been in charge of the ham room at the Shelbyville restaurant from the time that restaurant had been franchised. There is no one more qualified and knowledgeable about the preparation of old country ham than Fred. So it was only natural that he was placed in charge of this new undertaking.

Claudia says of him, "He is an expert on old country hams and prepares them just the way we want them prepared. Curing our hams ourselves insures uniform quality. Not only are the hams cured alike, they are prepared for serving in the kitchen of each restaurant in the same manner. This gives the customer the assurance of enjoying the same delicious old country ham dinner at any of the Claudia Sanders Dinner Houses no matter in what part of the country they are located."

Fred Settle, Jr., tells us, "The country ham business will be based at Cecilia, Kentucky. A lot of pigs are raised in that part of Kentucky and since hams are where the pigs are we want to be where the pigs are." He laughs as he says this and continues in a more serious vein. "We will ship hams to all the Claudia Sanders Dinner Houses from Cecilia. But we are not limiting the operation to merely supplying hams to the Claudia Sanders Dinner Houses. We will continue to fill

A view of just a few of the country hams at Claudia Sanders' plant at Cecilia, Kentucky. As many as 50,000 hams are cured here a year.

orders from customers all over the United States as we do now from Shelbyville, and will be able to do so on a much larger scale after the enterprise at Cecilia gets under way."

With all this activity in their lives it is easy to see why the Colonel and Claudia never developed a hobby.

"Our work is our hobby," Claudia says. "We probably enjoy our work more than most people enjoy their hobbies. Anyway, we enjoy our work so much it never seems like work to us."

Many circumstances in Claudia's have their parallel in the Colonel's life. She, like the Colonel, was born in the country and had known farm life, had helped rear her brothers and sisters as had the Colonel helped his mother with her two other children, had known hard work and the discipline of a saintly and compassionate mother, and had suffered the tragedy of divorce.

In 1975, Claudia found herself faced with what could prove to be a tragic visit to the hospital. Just about the time she was getting deeply involved with her two new projects, the franchising of her restaurants and the country ham business, she noticed she was beginning to have trouble with her eyes. A visit to the eye doctor disclosed she suffered from a detached retina. Due to the seriousness of the condition the doctor recommended an immediate operation and she was rushed to the hospital.

In like manner, in 1973, the Colonel had learned during a physical examination that an X-ray of his abdomen had disclosed what appeared to be a polyp in his colon. Since his operation could be safely postponed for a day or so, the Colonel had ample time to seek out a minister and ask for help from God.

"I knew God could heal me if I had enough faith," says the Colonel. "So I was not too surprised when the doctors told me after the operation they had been unable to find any evidence of a polyp."

But poor Claudia had no time to do what the Colonel was able to do. Her condition was such that it required immediate surgery. So, she prayed silently and asked that her sight be spared.

"I had no time to seek out a minister, nor go to a church to pray," she says. "All I could do was to pray to myself and hope that the

Lord would hear. He answered my prayers for the operation was a success and I have regained my sight with very little loss of vision. So, I guess it is not how nor where you pray but the sincerity of your prayers that counts."

A few years after this operation Claudia had a delightful new experience. She accompanied the Colonel on one of his trips, this time going around the world. This was a new experience for the Colonel, too, and they both enjoyed it immensely. Many of the places they visited were places they had been before. They spent ten days in Japan and later more than two weeks in Spain where the Colonel made some commercials for his Fried Chicken operation in Canada.

Claudia says, "The highlight of this around-the-world voyage was the stay in Iran. We stopped in Teheran where we were entertained royally by the local citizens who were connected with the Kentucky Fried Chicken business. We were taken to a garden party in the country which was a most colorful affair enhanced by the mingling of the dress and customs of the West with those of the Orient.

"Our stay in Teheran was quiet and peaceful although we did hear rumors of trouble and unrest in other parts of the city and in the country. At that time we had no idea that this was the beginning of what later was to grow into the trouble which faces the world today."

Asked about her plans for the future, Claudia smiles and says, "To speak for myself and the Colonel too, I might say that it doesn't seem necessary for us to make plans. Things just seem to happen in our lives. To me, there is something very enjoyable about that. It means that life is full of surprises and, for the most part, the surprises have been pleasant ones. Our lives, like the lives of everyone, have consisted of so much happiness and so much sadness, some failures and some successes, the good with the bad. The important thing is that we did not let adversity defeat us. Neither the Colonel nor I would have wanted an easy life. Most of the pleasure of living is in solving your problems and overcoming your obstacles."

Had their lives been easy ones, there might be no Claudia and

Colonel as we know them today. After all, it is the roughness of the sandpaper that smooths the wood and brings out its beauty.

Then too, the secret of their success might be summed up in one sentence: They kept their faith in God.

THE END

The Colonel dressed up in this Indian headdress to pose with Claudia while on vacation in Banff.

Claudia and the Colonel opening a present from one of the Colonel's grandchildren.

ABOUT THE AUTHOR

Edward G. Klemm, Jr.

Born in Louisville, Ky. 1910. Son of Roberta K. Klemm, a published poet and songwriter, and Edward G. Klemm, Sr., a Louisville attorney.

Graduated from University of Chicago in 1932. Taught in Louisville Junior and Senior High Schools and was a newspaper reporter before opening own real estate and insurance business in Louisville.

With his Mother, Roberta K. Klemm, has written music which has been published both in the United States and in Vienna, Austria.

Is a member of ASCAP, a Life Member of the National Association of American Composers and Conductors, a Life Member of the J.B. Speed Art Museum.

Has traveled extensively and sold photographs to magazines.

Three previously published books: "Precious Heritage", a novel, "I Wonder Why", a book of poems, and "The Claudia Sanders Dinner House Of Shelbyville, Kentucky, Cookbook".

On the following pages are some of Claudia's personal recipes. She tells us, "I love to cook and enjoy sharing some of my recipes with my friends. Remember in cooking that time is a valuable ingredient and no cooking should be hurried. Another valuable ingredient is the seasoning of the food and that is why we use only the spices and seasonings of the Marion-Kay company in all our recipes. Be sure to use them in the following recipes if you want the taste the Colonel and I enjoy in our own home."

BANANA BREAD

½ cup shortening
¾ cup sugar
2 eggs
¾ cup mashed bananas
1¼ cups sifted flour, (equal amounts white and whole wheat flour)
¾ teaspoon soda
½ teaspoon salt

Cream the shortening and sugar until light and fluffy. Stir in the bananas and eggs and then add the flour, soda and salt. Pour into a greased 9x9x2-inch pan bake at 350° for 30 to 35 minutes. Cut in squares and serve.

Roberta K. Klemm gave us this recipe which we enjoy very much.

FLUFFY BISCUITS

2 cups flour
2 tablespoons shortening
4 teaspoons baking powder
¾ cup milk
½ teaspoon salt

Sift flour, baking powder and salt together. Add the shortening and mix lightly with a fork. Then add the milk slowly. Handling as little as possible roll out mixture on a floured board to about 1-inch thick and cut with biscuit cutter first dipped in flour. Bake in hot oven, 400°, 12 or 15 minutes.

COLESLAW

3 cups shredded cabbage
1 tablespoon finely chopped onion
½ cup sour cream
1 tablespoon vinegar
½ teaspoon salt
¼ teaspoon black pepper

Thoroughly mix all ingredients and refrigerate before serving.

OYSTER SOUP

1 quart oysters
1 quart milk
2 tablespoons butter
1 teaspoon onion juice
½ teaspoon salt
¼ teaspoon pepper
1 tablespoon minced parsley

Strain the oysters. Heat the liquor in a saucepan but do not bring to a boil. Heat the milk in a double boiler and combine with the hot oyster liquor. Add the butter, seasoning and the oysters and cook until oysters puff and are crinkled at edges. Serve hot from the stove for best taste. Serves 6.

CURRIED TOMATO BISQUE

2 cans condensed tomato soup (10¾ ounce size. Undiluted)
¼ cup finely sliced green onions
2½ tablespoons melted butter
2½ cups water
¾ teaspoon curry powder
2 hard-cooked egg yolks, grated

Cook the onion in the butter until lightly browned. Add the water, tomato soup and curry powder and heat thoroughly. Stir constantly. Garnish with the grated egg yolk before serving.

CANDIED CARROTS

6 medium-sized carrots
½ cup water
1 cup brown sugar
4 tablespoons butter
¼ teaspoon cinnamon

Boil carrots. Scrape and cut into strips. Combine water, brown sugar, butter and cinnamon in a baking dish and cook to make a syrup. Place carrots in this syrup so they are completely covered and bake at 350° until candied. This should take about 20 minutes. Serves 6.

ROAST BEEF

1 5-pound roast
3 teaspoons salt
½ teaspoon black pepper
3 garlic cloves
flour

First, brown the roast on both sides in a skillet and rub well with the salt and pepper. Push the three garlic cloves well into the meat. Dredge meat with the flour and place on rack in roasting pan. Cook in 500° oven for about 20 minutes and then reduce heat to 300°. When roast is nearly done I like to put carrots, potatoes and onions around it and continue cooking until they and the roast are done.

OUR CHRISTMAS EGGNOG

6 eggs, separated
½ cup granulated sugar
2 cups light or whipping cream
2 cups milk
⅛ teaspoon salt
2 teaspoons vanilla
fresh ground nutmeg

Beat egg yolks and sugar until thick. Then add the cream, milk, salt and vanilla and beat well. Beat egg whites until they hold stiff peaks; fold into the yellow mixture. Garnish with nutmeg and serve chilled.

MY FAMILY'S FAVORITE BEETS

1 quart canned tiny beets
1 tablespoon vinegar
1 teaspoon salt
¼ cup fresh orange juice
½ cup sugar
1½ tablespoons cornstarch

Drain the beets, but save the juice from the can. Add the cornstarch to about ¼ the juice. Mix the vinegar, salt and orange juice with the rest of the beet juice and cook until it comes to a boil. Then add the cornstarch mixture and continue cooking until it thickens. Add the sugar and continue cooking until the sugar disolves. Add the beets and cook to heat thoroughly.

CORN PUDDING

2 cups creamed corn
2 well-beaten eggs
1¼ cups half and half
3 tablespoons flour
3 tablespoons butter
2 tablespoons granulated sugar
1 teaspoon salt
⅛ teaspoon black pepper

Melt the butter and combine with the flour, sugar, salt and pepper. Slowly add the half and half and stir in the corn. Add eggs and pour into well-buttered 1-quart casserole. Bake at 375° for 15 minutes and then lower to 350° and continue baking for about 30 minutes or until the mixture is set.